D0523990

HIDDEN
DORSET

Compiled by the Dorset
Federation of Women's Institutes from notes
sent by Institutes in the County

with illustrations by Pip Challenger

Published jointly by
Countryside Books, Newbury
and the D.F.W.I., Dorchester

First Published 1990
© Dorset Federation of Women's Institutes 1990

COUNTRYSIDE BOOKS
3 Catherine Road
Newbury, Berkshire

ISBN 1 85306 104 2

Produced through MRM Associates Ltd., Reading
Typeset by Acorn Bookwork, Salisbury
Printed in England by J. W. Arrowsmith Ltd., Bristol

Foreword

This is a selection of some of the lesser known history and tales of Dorset contributed by Women's Institute members fortunate enough to live in this beautiful and interesting County.

I would like to express my thanks to them for giving the opportunity to learn more of 'Hidden Dorset'. Also to County Secretary, Miss Sally Cave, for collating the entries and finally to the Editors of Countryside Books for producing it with the delightful pen and ink drawings by Pip Challenger.

I am sure you will enjoy reading this book and seeing some of the places mentioned – though perhaps not the ghosts!

Margaret E. Gibson
County Chairman

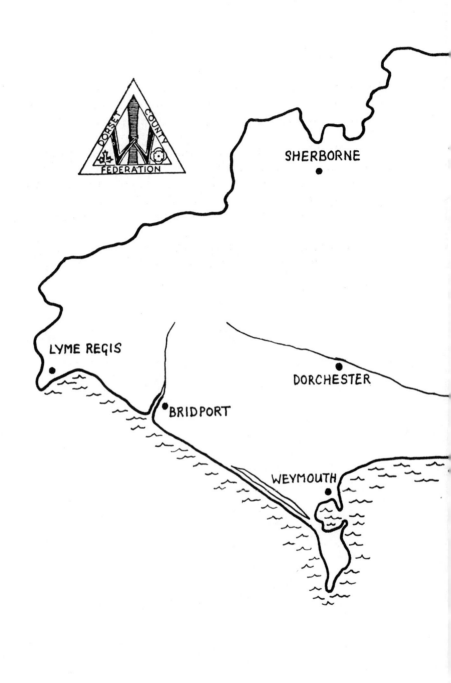

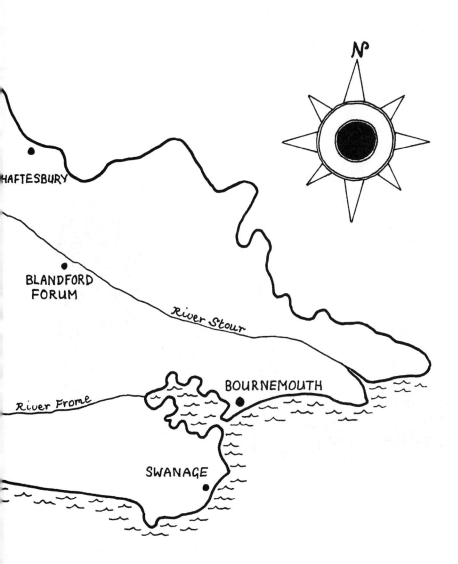

N

HAFTESBURY

BLANDFORD
FORUM

River Stour

River Frome

BOURNEMOUTH

SWANAGE

County of

DORSET

Monks' barn at Abbotsbury

Abbotsbury

Abbotsbury is one of the jewels of Dorset. The swannery and the monastic remains are an attraction for tourists, but you are lucky if you come here when it is quiet. Then the sense of history is almost tangible, and it is a delight to explore the buildings and ruins of many centuries.

Its name means Abbots' Town after the abbots of Glastonbury who held the land before King Canute granted it to his steward, Orc. Canute's successor, Edward the Confessor confirmed Orc's possession of the land and in 1044 gave consent to a monastery being built there by Orc, in which he installed Benedictine monks from Cerne Abbas.

Orc and his wife, Tola, spent much of their time acquiring land which they subsequently left to the monastery. One piece of land purchased by Tola was then called Tola's Piddle – we now know it as Tolpuddle, the home of the famous Martyrs.

The monks lived well. They had 14 acres, laid out mostly in gardens and fish ponds and they had the right to take the wild swans which frequented the lagoon nearby. They clipped the swans' wings and bred from them. A large decoy was used to catch wild fowl and they built a huge barn to house the supplies of grain etc from their extensive lands. They had a right to the wreck of the sea nearby and first choice of the fish caught there.

Their massive barn still stands, though half consists only of the outer walls. It is a truly impressive sight, nearly 300 ft long, and a striking reminder of the importance of the abbey.

After the Dissolution of the Monasteries in 1539, King Henry VIII granted Abbotsbury to Sir Giles Strangways and it has been in the ownership of his family ever since, apart from certain leasehold sales which have been made in recent years.

The monastery was adapted by Sir Giles to a private residence for periodic use – the family seat being at Melbury House, near Evershot. When the Civil War came, the Strangways and Abbotsbury were strongly Royalist and the house was made a Royalist garrison. By September 1644 the Roundheads were in control of most of Dorset and Sir Anthony Ashley Cooper then marched a large number of troops to Abbotsbury from Dorchester where they were encamped, to secure the surrender of the garrison. The Royalists would not surrender and a six hour battle ensued. There are still bullet holes in the Jacobean pulpit of St Nicholas' church.

The occupants of the garrison finally asked to surrender but Sir Anthony had lost a number of men and would not agree. He instructed his troops to burn the house down. He did not know that one of his captains at the back of the house had accepted the surrender and his own men were rushing into the house to plunder and loot.

By the time he realised what had happened, the house was well alight and although he called to his men to get out before the arsenal of gunpowder inside exploded, they did not heed. About 60 were blown up and killed. The house was burnt out, but one wall remains, near the church.

At one time Abbotsbury was infamous for its smuggling activities. No doubt the great barn hid many a smuggled load during the 18th century. St Catherine's tower, high on the hill, and the heights of Abbotsbury Castle hill fort, were ideal watching and signalling stations and would have been visible many miles out to sea. The smugglers' headquarters in the village was the Ilchester Arms, formerly known as the Ship.

Alderholt

➤ Alderholt is a large and growing village on the border of Dorset and Hampshire, two miles from Fordingbridge, on the edge of Cranborne Chase to the west and the New Forest to the east. The main village grew up in the 19th century around the railway station, then called Daggons Road. Originally it consisted of a number of widespread hamlets, covering one of the largest parishes in the county.

However, if you turn left off the Alderholt-Fordingbridge road, on a double bend beside Moonacre Cottage, (Pressey's Corner, taking its name from the bakery, which is now a restaurant), and continue under the old railway bridge, the road twists and turns past the entrance to Alderholt Park. Near here the original church stood some 200 years ago and a little further on the right is a lovely old thatched farmhouse, which stands back beside a small green and dates back to the 13th century. Continue on, up and down hill for a further half a mile and the signpost still has its finial stating 'Alderholt Mill'. Alderholt Mill farm is on the right opposite Bull Hill Lane and Alderholt Mill House. A few yards round the corner and there is the mill itself, standing back from the road with the stream gushing from under the building.

A very picturesque and hidden place, it stands on the site of a 14th century mill, then known as Padenor's Mill after the owner, William de Padenor. Records exist in the Salisbury estate accounts of the mill in 1330, when it was probably part of the Cranborne estate.

This was one of four mills on the river Allen/Ashford Water which runs into the river Avon in Fordingbridge. It is the only one remaining intact – Damerham is just a small cottage, Hawkhill is a farmhouse and the other has disappeared altogether.

Standing in a curve of drive, surrounded by water, the mill itself comes first, then a small annexe and the house that now goes with it, which was originally three cottages but was converted some 25 years ago when the mill was sold away from the mill house. The field behind is an old water meadow, serrated by ditches which after heavy rainfall fill up and create a herringbone effect. Some of these ditches originally had hatches on the millstream side, presumably to enable them to be flooded in the spring for an 'early bite'. The field is itself surrounded by water, the main stream going down one side, and a hatch at the top of the field controls the water down the millstream, which is manmade. Unlike most mills there is no pond or leat behind, only a small stream, and the water has to be built up to allow the wheel to work.

Many of the trees that surround the property are alders and willows and rumour has it that the stream used to be the home of otters – hence the name Alderholt.

The mill was used during the war for grinding cattle food, though locals say the tailrace was silted up between the wars. It remained standing idle until 1982, except when a previous owner used the power from the wheel to run a lathe. The wheel itself was originally inside the building, in the water running under the building, but it now stands behind the mill and is a massive iron wheel, made by Mundens of Ringwood in about 1840 (their name can be seen on the side). Water is diverted onto the wheel from the mill stream by closing a hatch under the main building and sending the water down over another hatch – it is a breast-struck wheel, slightly unusual, and the tailrace runs behind the house, joining the main stream before running under the bridge. When the present owner bought the property he was told by a local character he would now be 'King of Monkey Island'. This presumably came about because at one time 13 children lived in the cottages!

In 1982 it was found that the woodwork in the mill building needed treating for woodworm and deathwatch beetle. If it was to be preserved, a decision had to be made whether or not to preserve it and in view of the amount of machinery left, it was felt it would be a shame to let it go. The work was done and in order to continue with the restoration and make it self-financing it was opened to the public. The profits from the arts and crafts now exhibited have made it possible to continue to maintain the machinery and restore it to full working order. Milling of locally grown wheat started in 1987 and this has proved a popular attraction.

Ashley Chase

Inland from Abbotsbury is an area called Ashley Chase. The road by it has been demoted to a bridle path, but once it was a busy, much used road from Abbotsbury to Litton Cheney. A stream runs from the high ground, across a meadow, circling a small hill thick with hazel trees and hawthorn.

In the hedge beside the bridle path is a broken stile, with a steep path leading down to the stream. No bridge, it has to be jumped over. A scramble up the farther bank, through the undergrowth, with patches of bluebells and wood anemones, will bring you to the arched doorway of a ruined chapel, St Luke's chapel, once the property of Netley Abbey near Southampton.

Since the Dissolution of the Monasteries in the 16th century it has fallen into disrepair.

Only the western gable-end still stands, the roof and other three walls consisting now of densely-growing hazels and other trees. The first thing to catch your eye is a stone altar covered with moss. Sometimes there will be a small bunch of wild flowers on the altar in memory of the Milne-Watson family, who used to own the estate of Ashley Chase and who lived in Ashley House in the valley below. They are remembered on recumbent memorial stones in front of the altar.

Our records show that in medieval times Netley Abbey, a monastery on the banks of Southampton water, held the land at Ashley. It is safe to assume that the Cistercian monks from Netley began farming at Ashley sometime after the founding of the abbey in 1239 and that one of their first tasks would have been to build a chapel in which to worship.

Visit it in the spring when the bluebells provide a brilliant blue carpet to lead you into this ancient chapel with its timeless sense of peace.

St Luke's chapel ruins, Ashley Chase

Ashley Heath

Ashley Heath is situated in east Dorset, to the north of Bournemouth. It is a modern creation, planned as a garden village, and surprisingly it merits a mention in the Guinness Book of Records.

The area was at one time known as the Hampshire Heath Estate Project. It is only in recent years that Ashley Heath has been in the county of Dorset through government changes in boundary lines.

The reclaiming of waste land began in the early 1920s, inspired by a young statesman, Winston Churchill. When the land had been cleared of trees and heather, it was found to be very sandy and in places water-logged.

The land was fertilised at great cost and various crops were planted – potatoes, green crops, oats and wheat. Sheep and cows were grazed on specially planted areas of clover. Horses were brought in to work on the land and Mr Dymond, the blacksmith from Three Legged Cross, would come out to shoe them. Eventually a forge was built next to the railway line that ran from Ringwood through Ashley Heath, and on to West Moors and Ferndown to Poole. A walking and cycling lane now follows the line of the old track.

By 1928 further cultivation of the land was found to be too costly and so the land was designated for housing. The area was planted with trees and the Forestry Commission acquired a considerable amount of barren land to be planted with pine trees.

A builder was commissioned from Devon. First he built himself a house, with an office. This is now an hotel in Horton Road.

A High Street was built, containing four shops with bow windows, a clock tower and a cock weathervane. Under the clock face is the inscription 'The Night Cometh'. This is the

15

smallest high street in the country, and is mentioned as such in the Guinness Book of Records. A rose garden with a lily pond was laid out in the front of the shops, where teas were served.

Each bungalow was built on one acre of land. Unskilled labour was employed to keep the costs down, and one of the most expensive items was the roof covering. Tiles were very expensive and difficult to obtain. Eventually a cheaper corrugated tile was purchased from a firm in Holland. These properties can be found by travelling from the High Street into Woodbridge Road and Lions Lane.

The gardens were planted with shrubs and trees. The amelanchier shrub is especially attractive, with its white blossom in the spring and picturesque reds, yellows and oranges in the autumn.

After the Second World War the Old Forge was run by Miss Odell, who sold sweets, newspapers and petrol and kept a beautiful rose garden. She was so loved for her kindness to animals that a collection was made by the village on her retirement. Then the Old Forge was pulled down and a new building took its place, still retaining the name. It is still a sweet shop, and is also now the post office.

Ashley Heath is still growing, with new properties being built. There are pleasant walks in the nearby forests and a new country park is being developed along the Horton Road on what was formerly known as Kings Farm.

Ashmore

Ashmore is found in the Domesday Book under the name of Aismare, derived from the great pond or mere round which the village has grown up. It is seldom dry even in the very hottest season. At this pond the flocks no doubt would gather for drinking, when the downs were the home of the nomadic tribes who have left their mark in burial barrows as well as in flint weapons and tools. There is nothing quite like this pond anywhere in the neighbourhood, nor indeed in all the down country of Wiltshire and Dorset.

From time to time the pond goes dry; it is then the ancient custom of the villagers to hold a feast. Cakes are baked and eaten round the margin of the pond, and farmers haul out the hundreds of cart loads of mud that have accumulated in the bed and use it for manure. The pond is said to be 16 ft deep in the centre, and the last time it went dry was in 1921.

A strong local tradition concerns the Gabbergennies, or Gabbigammies. Many now living have been told by their forbears of the weird gibberings heard at night, down the Cow Leases to Washer's Pit, a dark lonely pond formerly overhung by great trees. Eventually the road was made to it and up Millway to the upper Blandford – Shaftesbury road. During the excavations, a human skeleton was found and was given Christian burial. Since then all noises have ceased. Older generations also spoke of 'It'. They said that on dark nights, when walking down to Washer's Pit, a woman in white was seen and felt brushing by them; something like a bale of wool seemed to be gently flopping down behind them, which set their hair on end.

There is another story connected with Washer's Pit, in which Squire Barber figured in the mid-18th century. Apparently, one night he dreamt that a woman was in distress at Washer's Pit. The dream was so real that it woke him. Summoning the household, he asked for volunteers to go and investigate. None would do so, but at length the cook, whose name was Mullins, said she would go if the Squire would lend her his best horse. This request being granted, off she went. On arriving at Washer's Pit, there was a woman hanging by her hair from a tree. Just as Mrs Mullins had cut the woman down and was preparing to ride home, she was set on by a band of men hiding in the woods. Managing to mount her horse and jumping a five-barred gate, she galloped off carrying the woman in front of her. Squire Barber was so pleased with her action that he gave her a cottage to live in and it has been known ever since as Mullins.

A source of income to the village folk in the past was the great autumn work of nutting, carried out by the women. Before foreign nuts were brought into the English market, there was a great demand for hazel nuts, and there was also a big market for unripe nuts as a 'mordant' by dyers. At a certain time in the autumn when it would least interfere with the game, the woods were thrown open to the villagers, and the women and girls dressed in long canvas overalls went out nutting. It was quite a village holiday, the girls often being accompanied by their swains, and much courting was done. The nuts when collected were sold to dealers, and in a good year would be worth about £400 to the villagers. This was perhaps exceptional, but half this amount would generally be reckoned on and this sum enabled the people to clear away their debt at the village shop or pay their rent.

Ashmore, in common with many other villages, used also to have its May Day revels. The village stocks stood against the wall of North Farm facing the side of the war memorial. The maypole stood about 40 ft south of the war memorial. One year these revels were perhaps rather more boisterous than usual with the result that the top of the maypole was cut off and thrown down the adjacent well, thus rendering it useless.

There was a certain amount of method in their madness. The well had been built in 1825 and cost about £50. It replaced the rain water cisterns which had served the village until then as their water supply. The well was over 300 ft deep and entailed much hard work in drawing water, so the villagers put the maypole in the well and returned happily to their rain water butts!

Batcombe

Although Batcombe Down itself is by no means hidden, this beautiful area has a great deal to be discovered. The lovely ridge of chalk hills runs from Holywell in the west to High Stoy in the east. To the north-east lies Blackmore Vale with its blue mists, or, on clear days, spectacular views to the Mendips, Quantocks and Exmoor. On the south side there are rolling chalk downs to Cerne Abbas and Dorchester.

Nowadays there is a simple but well laid out picnic area on the summit of the hill, with footpaths zigzagging on the north side through the hazel groves and conifers. At the vale's edge is Flowers Farm, a very well run establishment with a warm welcome for any who may call, for this is the home of the Franciscan Brothers. Not far away on the chalky, precipitous down is a Site of Special Scientific Interest, where seven species of orchids grow undisturbed by cultivation.

The tiny village of Batcombe is now just a light scattering of farmsteads and cottages. The church is near the bottom of the down, which surrounds it closely on three sides.

The church tower has only three pinnacles, but legend says that once there were four. The story goes that Squire John Minterne (otherwise known as 'Conjuring Minterne') jumped his horse from the crest of the hill into the village below, the horse's hoof knocking the fourth pinnacle asunder as they floated over the church. John Minterne's tomb can be seen in the churchyard. Whether the legend is true or not, the location of the church certainly gives scope to the imagination.

Back on the hilltop, in a desolate spot near the road between Minterne and Holywell, is an ancient stone known as 'The Cross in Hand'. This pillar, with what appears to be a clenched hand or bowl at the top, has given rise to many legends over the centuries. How long it has stood here no-one knows. Thomas Hardy used it in *Tess of the D'Urbervilles*

'The Cross in Hand', Batcombe

when describing Tess's long trek to Beaminster. Alec makes Tess put her hand on the stone when she promises never to tempt him. Hardy's shepherd described it as a 'thing of ill omen'. More prosaically, it was probably erected as some kind of boundary marker.

Batcombe is an area of outstanding natural beauty, yet at times can be cold and desolate. From the valley its changing moods can be clearly seen. In winter time if there is any snow about, it will always linger longer at Batcombe than anywhere else in sight.

Beaminster

➤ Near the old-world town of Beaminster (the Emminster of Hardy's *Tess of the D'Urbervilles*), amid the highlands of Dorset, is a little graveyard known as 'Daniel's Knowle', a romantic spot standing alone in its solitude.

The tiny but historic cemetery was the burial place of the Daniels of Beaminster for more than two centuries.

James Daniel, an attorney at law, was born in 1611 and lived in a house in Hogshill Street, Beaminster. A house and antique shop is now on this site, called 'Daniel's House'. At the age of 74 he fought on Monmouth's side at Sedgemoor. When Monmouth was defeated James Daniel escaped and came back to his home in Beaminster.

Being a man of considerable influence, a substantial reward was offered for his capture. The fugitive therefore decided to seek shelter in a barn at Knowle Farm and concealed himself beneath some straw. Although soldiers diligently searched the premises, he remained undiscovered.

In after years when the heat of persecution had subsided and when the men of the West could talk in safety about the memory of Monmouth and with indignation of the horrors of the Bloody Assize, the barn at Knowle was removed and the land made into a family burial ground. James Daniel himself was the first to lie there, at the age of 100, and after that all Daniel descendants who died in the neighbourhood were buried there. The ground was not consecrated, however, until 1860, as the Daniels were nonconformists.

As Knowle Farm belonged to the Daniels it was part of the tenant farmer's duty to care for the burial ground. In 1956 the farm was sold and went out of the family's ownership and one could not expect the present owner to keep the burial ground in order. It is still there but as it is on private ground permission would have to be obtained from the present owner to visit it. On several occasions different groups have tidied the little burial ground.

On a quiet, secluded hilltop half a mile to the south of Beaminster, over the fields towards Netherbury, there is another unusual grave. The 'Airman's Grave' is the resting place of Lt William Rhodes-Moorhouse, who was killed in action in 1915.

He was the first airman ever to receive the VC, which was awarded posthumously. He was severely wounded while on a bombing raid over Courtrai in France. He managed to fly his aircraft back to his French base at Merville, but died of his wounds the following day. Special permission was given for his body to be brought home, and he was buried with due ceremony in a grave lined with spring flowers. The area was enclosed with iron railings and a garden was made in the shape of an aeroplane and planted with forget-me-nots. The grave is kept up by local people and the forget-me-nots are still planted every year.

William was buried on the hilltop because it was a special place to him. He had intended to build a summer house there, where he could command a panoramic view of Beaminster to the north, Netherbury to the south, and to the east, his beloved home, the beautiful Tudor manor house of Parnham, now occupied by the John Makepeace Workshops. In William's day there was an avenue of trees from Parnham House to the hilltop, traces of which can still be seen today.

William was born in 1887 and had been involved in aviation all his adult life, having at one time built his own aeroplane. His wife, Linda, was a pilot and his only son, also named William, was a pilot in the Second World War and was awarded the DFC. He was killed in action in 1940. Their ashes are interred at the Airman's Grave.

The site is well worth a visit and on a sunny day the peace and tranquillity of the place has to be experienced to be believed. Access to the grave is easy as there are footpaths from Southgate and from St Mary Well Street over the fields to Netherbury, and another footpath from the Beaminster to Bridport road along the drive to Parnham House, continuing straight on between the house on the left and outbuildings on the right, to a downhill path leading to a bridge over the river. Crossing the river, the path bears slightly right and uphill through woodland to join up with the footpath to Netherbury. Turn left towards Netherbury and the Airman's Grave is on the hilltop on the right, approached via a stile leading into the field.

Beaminster itself is full of interest. The Old Vicarage, for instance, is a listed building and a prime example of High Victorian Gothic architectural style. It was built between 1859 and 1861 for the Reverend Alfred Codd, then vicar of Beaminster, whose son, Alfred Percy Codd, talks about his childhood at the house in his booklet, *Life in Beaminster*.

In those days, the house, built of stone with a tiled roof, was a very fine building, gabled at the front and with dormer windows at the back. Set above the town in a spacious garden, there are fine views from the upper windows down towards the church and up towards the surrounding hills. It is unusual as a vicarage in that it is at a distance from the church, and, indeed, hardly looks as if it were ever connected with it; but during Alfred Codd's childhood the field between the vicarage and the church was the scene of the School Feast when flags were attached to the railings between the vicarage lawn and the field. These railings are still to be found sandwiched between a fir hedge and an interwoven fence, but the field has made way for Glebe Court and private housing in Barnes Lane.

For many people nowadays, the Old Vicarage's attraction lies in its literary associations as the 'Emminster vicarage', the family home of Tess's husband, Angel Clare, in *Tess of the D'Urbervilles*. Towards the end of the novel, Tess determines to go to the vicarage to ask for news of Clare. There is a moving description of her pausing at the top of Hackthorn

Hill to look down on to the town. On arrival at the vicarage, she finds no one to answer to her knocking; it is Sunday and the family are still at church, so Tess returns the way she has come. Later in the book, Angel Clare returns home and is silhouetted against the setting sun as he approaches the vicarage porch. It is known that Hardy did visit the vicarage and discussed certain particulars with Reverend Codd.

The Old Vicarage remained a vicarage until the mid 1970s. It stood empty for seven years in a delapidated state. It was cold, draughty and riddled with dry rot. With the development of the glebe lands, the building was sold and renovated for use as a private residence and an office for a computer company. The house itself continues to attract guests, who enjoy their bed and breakfast in its peaceful atmosphere.

Bincombe

Leaving the road from Dorchester to Weymouth along the Roman way and descending the Ridgeway with its fabulous views of the sea, a sharp turn to the left brings you to the small hamlet of Bincombe.

Few people notice the signpost with its direction to the east which leads to Holy Trinity church. Of Early English origin and still used for Anglican services, this peaceful place has a Norman font of Purbeck marble mounted on a pedestal of rough stone.

The church was given by William the Conqueror to the monastery of St Stephen of Caen in France. Indeed an entry in the Domesday Book, referring to an earlier reference to the abbey at Caen, states 'The same church holds Beincombe. Earl Harold held it in King Edward's time and it was taxed for eight hides'. Both Richard I and Henry IV confirmed the possession of the manor to Caen but after the suppression of alien houses it was given to the College of St Stephen, Westminster.

After several changes the manor and church benefice were bought by Gonville and Caius College, Cambridge, who with a college representative and choir come down from Cambridge and hold Sunday services in this remote and tiny church at regular intervals, as they still hold the advowson.

During the Napoleonic wars a large military camp was formed on Bincombe Down. It is said locally that the York Hussars stationed there, trained and marched up and down the steep hill near the church, inspiring the well known nursery rhyme;

'The Grand Old Duke of York,
He had ten thousand men,
He marched them up to the top of the hill,
And he marched them down again'.

Be that as it may, what is true is that outside Holy Trinity church, to the east of the chancel, are the unmarked graves of two Germans who were shot for desertion from the York Hussars. Their sad plight inspired Dorset poet and novelist Thomas Hardy to write *The Melancholy Hussar*.

Though the tiny hamlet may in the past have echoed to marching feet, today peace and quietness is enshrined in this corner of Dorset, where the famous Dorset White poll sheep safely graze in tranquillity.

Blandford Forum

➤ You do not have to visit the church to find a memorial to the men who, more than any others, had an effect on this lovely town. The men in question were brothers – John and William Bastard – and their work is all around you.

John and William were perhaps fortunate in that a terrible fire in 1731 destroyed much of old Blandford and presented them with an architect's dream – a blank canvas on which to create a town anew. The family firm of architects and builders were already well established locally, and were the natural choice to undertake such a huge project.

The fire had raged out of control for over five hours, despite the valiant efforts of the townspeople. Thatched buildings went up like tinder in the strong wind, and finally even the church succumbed to the flames. Fourteen people died and the devastation was complete.

It was customary then, as now, to make appeals for help when disaster of any kind struck a community. Throughout the country, appeals were made from church pulpits and collections organised, and money began to flow into Blandford. King George II gave £1,000 to the disaster fund. With this money the brothers were able to begin designing and building a new town.

Much of what they built is unchanged today, and Blandford presents a coherent Georgian face to the world. Private houses, the church, the grammar school and the town hall are all their work. In the Market Square is the town pump, which is inscribed 'In Grateful Acknowledgement of the Divine Mercy, that has raised this town, like the Phoenix from its ashes, to its present beautiful and flourishing state.' It is dated 1760 and was probably the last item to be built. It is a laudable affirmation of a determination that such a disaster should never again overtake Blandford, for it was intended to provide a head of water for any future firefighting.

At No. 38 Salisbury Street is a plaque recording that this was the home of Alfred Stevens, the painter and sculptor. Alfred was born in Blandford in 1818, the son of a housepainter and decorator. His early promise was recognised by the rector of Blandford St Mary, Samuel Best, who helped to send the young boy to Italy to study art. Alfred used his time well, travelling from city to city, learning as he went. In 1841 he became the pupil of the Danish sculptor Thorvaldsen in his studio in Rome. When he returned to England he got a job teaching architectural design at the School of Design in South Kensington.

Alfred believed that any object, no matter how humble its use, should be beautiful. He put this principle into practice as he designed anything and everything, from fire-dogs to railway carriages. Perhaps the crowning achievement of his career was to be chosen to design the monument to the Duke of Wellington in 1856, though the work was not completed until after his death in 1875. He was recognised as one of the great artists of his day. He had certainly travelled a long way from his origins in the little town of Blandford.

Bothenhampton

From Bridport's Sea Road, a lovely shady lane leads up and up to Bothenhampton. Once spelled, and sometimes still pronounced, Baunton, this picturesque little hilltop village has two unusual features, besides its wonderful views.

The first is the High Pavement, which rises from about one foot in height at the beginning of the lane to twelve feet or more. Through the main street it continues, rising and falling until finally it comes to ground level. Here in the high street the village has a little shop and post office, which has served the community well for many years, as did the George and the Royal Oak, the latter inn now a private residence. There are a few buildings on the other side of the road, where in the old days there were three farms with cottages.

The second feature is its two churches, both well worth exploring. You will soon see the church of Holy Trinity, set above the village as though keeping watch over it. It was consecrated in 1890, so is Bothenhampton's New Church, and its interest lies in the connection with the Arts and Crafts Movement of the late 19th century.

The church was designed by Edward S. Prior, a pupil of

William Lethaby. Prior had been involved in the foundation of the Art Workers' Guild, to bring together those associated with the creation of buildings, no matter where their skills lay. Holy Trinity is an impressive example of his original talent, with its deeply recessed windows and sweeping transverse arches. The altar frontal, often covered by the altar cloth, is by Lethaby himself, and is decorated in painted gesso. It is believed to have been exhibited at the Arts and Crafts Exhibition of 1889.

The Old Church served the community for some six centuries before parishioners decided it was too small, and too decayed, for their needs.

In the 13th century nearby Loders was a priory of the abbey of St Mary at Montburgh in Normandy, and Bothenhampton was a chapel of ease. Subsequently control of the priory passed to the nunnery of Syon at Twickenham. Births and deaths were still registered at Loders until 1733, when the chapel was transferred to Walditch.

The Old Church is now in the care of the Redundant Churches Fund and restoration repairs were carried out in the 1970s. All that remains today is the 14th century chancel, with its 18th century sanctuary, the 15th century tower and a little corner of the nave. The walled-in village burial ground surrounds the church and has been a quiet resting place for many villagers, situated as it is under Bothen Hill and wood, away from the humdrum of village life.

Fifty yards from Old Holy Trinity is the old school, where the village children learned their tables and to read and write. Not half a mile away was the Potteries, where a company carried on the art of brickmaking, supplying many places in the area. These bricks were used in the building of the church hall and clubroom in the main street of the village. Old quarries were also in use until early in the 20th century, the stone extracted being used for local paving and buildings. How sad that such local industries have gone for ever.

Bournemouth

➤ In the churchyard of St Peter's, marked by a white tombstone, is the communal grave of an extraordinary family. Here lie buried Mary Woolstonecraft Shelley, the author of *Frankenstein*; her parents, Mary Woolstonecraft and William Godwin; the heart of her husband, the poet Shelley; and their son.

Mary's mother, Mary Woolstonecraft, was born in 1759 in London. She worked as a governess and then as a translator and writer, and became a part of the fermenting world of politics, art and reform of the late 18th century. In 1792 she wrote *A Vindication of the Rights of Woman*, and incurred the wrath of many establishment figures by her advocacy of the equality of men and women. Horace Walpole called her a 'hyena in petticoats' for her views.

After observing first hand the 'Terror' of the Revolution in Paris, and a tragic love affair which almost ended in her suicide, Mary met William Godwin, a well known political writer. In 1797 they married and their daughter was born the same year. Less than two months later Mary was dead.

Godwin was the idol of several of the Romantic poets, including Wordsworth and Coleridge, and later young Mary was to meet Shelley in his circle. They scandalised polite society by their attitude towards 'free love' and their travels in Italy with a group of like-minded friends. It was during this time, in 1818, that *Frankenstein* was written.

In 1822 Shelley was drowned at sea off Italy. In a farewell intended to echo that for a Greek hero, his friends cremated his body on a funeral pyre on a beach not far from where his boat had gone down. However, it appears that his heart was not burned but was rescued from the fire by one of his friends, Edward Trelawney. Later it was given to his widow, Mary, who kept it by her to the end of her days, apparently wrapped in a copy of Shelley's *Adonais*. Mary Shelley spent many of her later years at local Boscombe Manor, the country home of her son, who inherited the baronetcy in 1844.

When Mary died in 1851 she was buried here at St Peter's. Her parents' bodies were brought here from their original resting place in Old St Pancras' churchyard and reburied with their daughter. Shelley's heart was also later interred, and when they were eventually joined by their son and his wife, this extraordinary family was complete. It is strange to think how much passion and poetry is buried here in the peace of St Peter's.

Briantspuddle

Sir Ernest Debenham was a philanthropist who wanted to use some of the money he had gained in his London shop, Debenham and Freebody, for the benefit of people and agriculture. His dream was to create an ideal village and he chose Briantspuddle, because it was a place which had neither especially good soil nor especially bad. He bought the estate in 1914 from the Framptons. His work in agriculture gained him his title and his dairy and pig farming was extremely up to date for this time. Some of his methods are still being used today.

The village was in rather poor straits when he came and he greatly improved the life of the villagers. He brought piped water to the village and during the winter months when there was not so much work on the land, he had the workers' co-operation in building new, solid cottages. A Scandinavian architect designed the cottages but the actual blocks, made with cement and gravel, were made in a tin bath by the villagers themselves. When they had made enough blocks, a cottage was built. The thatcher worked for Sir Ernest after he had worked for James Frampton in the same trade. All these cottages were thatched and a credit to the village.

Sir Ernest also instituted a forestry scheme in Briantspud-

Briantspuddle's war memorial, designed by Eric Gill

dle, where young men were apprenticed and taught the art of forestry under the auspices of Ursula Waterhouse, who was a pupil of St Barbe Baker, the original 'Man of the Trees'. Sir Ernest's granddaughter still owns some of the woods here.

The war memorial was designed by Eric Gill. It was originally to be a village cross, but was not actually finished until after the First World War, when it became a war memorial. It is a most unusual design, with a mother feeding her baby on one side and a stylized soldier with a sword on the other. The village children love to look at the mother and often play on the steps around the memorial.

Everybody who lived here had a job on the estate: farm workers, motor engineers who looked after the fleet of vehicles; the thatcher, the beekeeper who supplied the 'big house' with honey and sold the rest for his own profit, dairymaids, the carter who drove weekly to Dorchester and carried goods, parcels, animals and people, the river watcher for the water meadows, and many others. Milk was sold to the villagers, who bought coupons for this and then exchanged the coupons for milk at the dairy. Buttons were made from milk residues. The head dairyman had a large detached house next to the dairy block, now turned into residents' bungalows.

The village hall was built as a barn in 1803. Sir Ernest Debenham converted this into use as a meeting place and built on the kitchen at the back. The cob building is lofty and thatched. The village still has a set of Bladen estate crockery which was made specially for the 21st birthday party of Piers Debenham, the eldest son. A set of this crockery is in Dorchester Museum. Around the hall there is a collection of paintings by Sir Ernest's sister, Alison, who later became Madame Leplat. She was a student at the Slade School. The pictures are of the workers in the village and are said to be very good likenesses. There is Charles Payne the river watcher, John Fooks the thatcher, George Courtney the waggoner, George Trevitt the woodman, Robert Farr the farm bailiff, and Walter Goldring the water meadow man.

Next to the village hall is the Old Granary – a rather unusual building. One old couple spent their honeymoon there!

Briantspuddle is in the parish of Affpuddle. Affpuddle school had two classrooms only and in 1960 there were 39 children attending. During the Second World War 100 children were evacuated to the village from Southampton. The school was sponsored by James Frampton, son of the Frampton who had the Tolpuddle Martyrs condemned to exile. One of the builders was James Hammett, son of one of the Tolpuddle Martyrs. It is now a private house.

Briantspuddle has a great many trees but one is special. It is an oak standing by itself by the roadside, a hundred yards from the crossroads.

It is a beautiful tree, strong and sturdy, as beautiful during the winter when the branches, stark etched against the sky, are bare of leaves, as in the spring when the bronze buds are forming, or summer when the foliage is heavy and gives welcome shade, or again in autumn when the leaves turn to bronze and gold.

It was a great day when the sapling was planted. The school children and the village folk gathered around, and were told that far away in London King George VI was being crowned with great ceremony – in 1937.

The oak is already magnificent. King George VI is long since dead; his daughter has taken his place, but the tree still stands, a living memory of the day when a king was crowned. Do today's children passing by give a thought as to why one stately oak stands alone by the roadside when the other lanes are lined with trees? There is a plaque which gives the history of the tree, but the brambles and Queen Anne's Lace almost hide it.

In 1987 the parish of Affpuddle was 1,000 years old. Some stone was taken from beside the river which had been part of old Weymouth Bridge. This was worked by a sculptor from Purbeck into a commemorative stone and this stone is to be placed near the Coronation Tree, where these two, the living and the stone, will be reminders of the passing of time.

Bridport

Bridport's wide main streets and long alleys are a permanent reminder of the history of this bustling town. Rope and net making have been a part of local life since before the days of King John, when the hemp first introduced by the Romans was spun into yarn as a cottage industry to supply the local fishing boats.

Bridport's rope was in great demand – Henry VII decreed that all the hemp grown in a five mile radius of the town was to be kept exclusively for the use of the navy. It had other uses too. A 'Bridport Dagger' was the hangman's rope!

The late 18th century rope and net factory still stands in West Street, and the museum has an example of an 1830s net-making machine amongst its other informative displays. But it is perhaps the width of the streets and the layout of its adjoining rope walks which are most evocative of a time when nearly everyone in the town depended on the industry for their livelihood.

Space was needed for the making of rope. One end would be fastened to a spindle, the handle turned by a boy, whilst the rope-maker, with hemp wound round his body, walked backwards, drawing out the hemp with his hands and feeding the machine. Donkeys were used for the heavy work of polishing the completed rope.

Bridport was the centre of a widespread rope and twine making industry. 'Twine work' kept many women and unemployed men at work in the surrounding villages in the winter, when agricultural work and related trades were at their quietest. 'Net-breding' (net making or braiding) was taught in local schools. It was poorly paid work. Agents or carriers would buy the string from the villagers and bring it into Bridport, but in many cases they did not pay for it in cash. Instead they took orders for goods, such as clothing or boots, which they would deliver on the next trip. Not surprisingly, many villagers found this an expensive way of buying goods, but few could afford to do anything about it.

Broadoak

➤ The little village of Broadoak, in the parish of Symondsbury, nestles in the Marshwood Vale, to the north-west of Bridport. To its little church of St Paul's goes the honour of tending a treasured set of communion plate.

In the 19th century a cattle disease – the Kinderpest – swept the continent of Europe. The virus spread to Kent, then throughout the south-east, and everywhere the cattle died; there was no cure.

The people of Symondsbury – all connected with farming in one way or another – watched helplessly as the dreaded disease came closer.

There was only one thing to do – to go to the church and pray that they might be spared the hazard. Daily someone was in the church praying, and daily the Ritterbund Kinderpest swept closer.

When the disease reached Bridport and West Bay on the Symondsbury boundaries, suddenly it veered north by Salwayash before pursuing its westward path, and then turned south again beyond the western edge of the parish boundaries. Not one of the cattle contracted the disease or died: the prayers of the community had been answered.

When immunity had been assured, people went to the church for a thanksgiving service. To show their gratitude in a lasting manner, the lovely communion set was bought by the parishioners, suitably inscribed and given to St Paul's.

A love of the church is deep in the heart of every Symondsbury-born parishioner and still evokes willing service – local people do not forget.

Bryanston

Until 1927, when it became a boys public school, Bryanston House was lived in by the Portman family. They bought the estate in 1685 and for 200 years lived in a large house close to the river. In the 1890s a new house, the present school, was built by Norman Shaw for the 2nd Viscount Portman, and the stones of the old house were used to build a new church, St Martin's. The old church became the Portman Chapel, with many memorials of the family.

The Portmans were held in great affection by the village and stories of them still abound. Deer used to roam the park and white peacocks were bred on the estate. The eyes on their tail feathers were said to resemble watermarks. There was a legend that if ever the peacocks left Bryanston, the Portmans too would go. Oddly, it came true. The 3rd Viscount got rid of the peacocks, and shortly afterwards he died. The house and part of the estate were sold out of the family.

It was William Portman who captured the fugitive Duke of Monmouth after the disaster of Sedgemoor in 1685. Found hiding in a field ('Monmouth's Close') about two miles from Horton, he handed his sword over to Sir William. The sword for a long time had pride of place in the hall of Bryanston House.

There are still many beautiful trees in and around Bryanston, but the walnut trees were unfortunately cut down and sold in the early 20th century. During the Crimean War, the 1st Viscount Portman had been offered £50 a tree by the government, who wanted the wood to make gun stocks. His lordship declined!

A tale is told of Sir William Portman, who tried to fool his own jester. The jester, who seems to have annoyed Sir William in some way, was given a note to take to Dorchester, to be delivered to the constable at the gaol. Perhaps he was suspicious, or merely unwilling to walk the 16 miles into Dorchester, for the jester entrusted the note to a passing chimney sweep. Sir William was startled to find his jester still on the estate some hours later, and finally the story came out. A groom had to be sent immediately galloping off to Dorchester, for the note had read: 'Please lock this man up for 24 hours'!

Burton Bradstock

➤ On the outskirts of Burton Bradstock there is an inlet where the river Bride meets the sea, known as Burton Freshwater. A born and bred Burtoner will tell you that the dip in the hill leading from the present Burton Road down to the holiday complex, is called 'Red Bottom'.

When the Danes were mounting raids at various points along the Dorset coast, one unlucky party had the temerity to nose their longships into Burton Freshwater. Climbing the grassy dip in search of victims and plunder, they were taken unawares by a horde of savage Burtoners. The dip, it is said, ran red with Danish blood.

Legend does not explain how the invaded were ready for the invaders. Probably the men of Burton, as they had done since time immemorial (and indeed continued to do until the first quarter of the 20th century), would have had a lookout stationed on the clifftop to catch any sign of 'mackel strayen' and he, with his fisherman's keen eyesight, would have had ample time to warn the village.

Burtoners have had their eyes turned to the sea to watch for invaders in later centuries too. During the years prior to Trafalgar, every man, woman and child along the south coast lived in dread of invasion by Napoleon. Detailed preparations were made in case the enemy should appear. On the hills, such as nearby Shipton Hill, beacons were kept in readiness, to be fired immediately there came news of a landing. Plans were drawn up for action in case the invasion came.

The men (and women) of Burton Bradstock were no slouches when it came to defending their land. The local volunteers even had their own song, suitably stirring, one verse of which ran as follows:

> 'Lives that are lent for laws and King
> When that they may need 'em;
> Let us then in chorus sing
> Give us death or freedom.
> Chorus: To the field of Mars advance,
> Join the bold alliance!
> Tell the blood stain'd Sons of France
> We bid them all defiance.'

Given the fate of those Danes long ago, perhaps the French can be thankful they never tried to land in that little inlet at Burton Freshwater.

Charmouth

➤ The Domesday village of Charmouth straddles the old Roman road from Dorchester to Exeter. There is hardly a textbook dealing with geological rocks, stratigraphy or fossils, published anywhere in the world, that does not mention Charmouth! Visitors flock to the beach to search for fossils and to enjoy the wonderful coastal views. But there

The 'Lookout' at Charmouth

are other, lesser known, attractions in this ancient village.

Through the centre of the village the old road is called The Street. A prominent inn in The Street had been known all this century as 'the Star', with an inn sign appropriately illustrating its name. Many of the older customers, however, occasionally referred to it as the 'Drum and Monkey'. When the puzzled landlord queried this strange name, they said that this was what they had often heard their fathers calling it. With his interest now aroused, the landlord researched the whole background to the inn.

He found that the premises had first been used as an inn around 1640, and that it had originally been run by a retired naval officer. Later records also revealed that the inn was much frequented by seamen during Nelson's time. Whereas the navy's ships used to be sailed by a crew of seamen, most of the fighting was done by marines. The marines were smartly uniformed, and used to beat their drums, both when on board ship and when marching ashore. The biggest of all the drums was known as the 'Ship's Drum', and this was an important item of the ship's equipment. When a naval engagement took place, the heavy, muzzle-loading iron cannon were brought into play. The cast-iron cannon-balls were always neatly stacked alongside each gun but, for obvious safety reasons, the gunpowder was stored in a central magazine. It was the job of so-called 'Powder Monkeys', often young lads, to keep each gun supplied with gunpowder charges from this magazine.

Very pleased with the results of his researches, and gratified to have found the explanation for a most unusual inn name, the landlord changed the name back to the original Drum and Monkey in May 1988. The old inn sign depicting the Star was replaced by a new sign specially painted by a Yeovil artist, and bearing the revived name. Standing by a cannon on the deck of a naval vessel is portrayed one of the gun team with a ramrod, and more importantly a splendidly uniformed marine with his drum, and a young powder monkey standing by for action.

Visitors to Charmouth are also often puzzled by an unusual, octagonal-shaped building which stands on the crumbling edge of a low cliff above the foreshore and beach, near the mouth of the river Char. The walls are of the soft local stone, and have been rendered as a protection against the weather. There is a timber door on the more sheltered landward side, and windows are set in the three seaward walls – one facing south-east to command a view along the Chesil Beach and towards the Isle of Portland; another facing south across Lyme Bay and out to the Channel; and the third facing south-west towards the Cobb harbour at Lyme Regis. This unusual building is 'The Lookout'.

It was built by the Customs & Excise Service in 1804, at a time when England took the threat of a Napoleonic invasion very seriously. The south-east coasts were the ones thought to be most at risk from a sally by the French from their great port at Boulogne, but in addition to the redoubling of vigilance at the Cinque Ports, preparations were made all the way along the south and south-west coasts. An observation and warning system of lookout and signal posts was established at prominent points along the shoreline, together with beacons on the highest hills inland, all designed to enable invasion warnings to be flashed across the country with great speed and urgency. The invasion, however, never came.

Nevertheless, smuggling had for some time been rife along this coastline and, during the first half of the 19th century, the Lookout was used very effectively by the Excise & Coastguard Service in their endeavours to intercept the running of brandy from France, and to apprehend the smugglers. There is still a sunken lane running inland from the eastern cliffs of Charmouth which retains its earlier name of the Smugglers' Path. The *Western Flying Post* reported that one Saturday night in January 1825, three men of the Lyme Preventive Station were on the look-out near the mouth of the Charmouth river, where they captured 150 kegs and two men. But they were then discovered and attacked by 70–80 drunken smugglers who, in the struggle that followed, made off again with most of the brandy, leaving behind three of their number who subsequently served three months in Dorchester gaol. The registers of Dorchester gaol recorded similar imprisonments of Charmouth smugglers, including 21 year old Elizabeth Powell in 1824, and a 49 year old seaman, Henry Tippen, in 1828.

In 1856, the Excise & Coastguard Services were formally

taken over by the Admiralty, who continued to rent the Lookout and its adjacent flagstaff from the lord of the manor for £3 a year. In 1909, the use of the Lookout as an observation post was discontinued, and in 1945 the building was given to Charmouth Parish Council. In 1989, it was designated as a Grade II listed building by the Department of the Environment. As it is rented out annually to a local resident, like many of the nearby beach huts, it has been said that Charmouth has the only 'listed' beach hut in the country!

On his death in 1661, a retired Charmouth mariner named Anthony Tutcher bequeathed a one acre field, on which stood a house, for the benefit of needy seamen and seamen's wives and children. He instructed that the charity was to be administered by the rector and a Board of Trustees, and that the income from this property was to be laid out in stockings and shoes to be provided for the needy beneficiaries. The plot of land was on the west side of Sea Lane – or Lower Sea Lane as it is now called – and it soon became known in the village as 'Stocking and Shoe Land'. During the following centuries the name often became transposed into 'Shoe and Stocking'. Two adjoining dwellings known as Woodcote and Greengates, now stand on the plot.

The original aims of the charity were later varied, probably because the number of needy seamen and their families had steadily diminished in the village. There had been a parish almshouse on the northern side of The Street, opposite where the Royal Oak now stands, in which there were three rooms downstairs, and three upstairs. The almshouse provided homes for poor soldiers and sailors, of whom there were six in residence in 1836. Four of these were being assisted by parish relief after having been transferred here in 1820 from the parish poor house in Old Lyme Hill, where now stand the two cottages St Gabriels and Silver.

The income from the 'Stocking and Shoe Land' was now applied to repair and maintain the almshouse, any left over being more than ample to continue with the provision of stockings and shoes for needy seamen and their dependents.

Adjacent to the almshouse were three cottages which, in the 1850s, were bought by a Mrs Napier Stuart of Harley Street, London, who owned much land in Charmouth. She resolved to knock these three cottages down and build in their place a superior residence she proposed to call 'The Court'. Feeling that the rather dilapidated almshouse spoilt the setting for The Court, she offered to purchase another plot of land in Sea Lane, remove a butcher's slaughter-house that stood on it, and build two new almshouses there. The Parish Council accepted the offer, and in 1868 the new almshouses were built on the east side of Sea Lane just below where the school now stands. The six occupants of the old almshouses were resettled into the new ones, enabling Mrs Stuart to demolish the old building and replace it by a coach-house and stables for The Court.

In 1921, following an application to the Charity Commissioners, the Stocking and Shoe Charity and seven other lesser charities were amalgamated into the Charmouth United Charities. This is still administered by a Board of Trustees, giving assistance to about 30 deserving villagers, mainly in the form of fuel and food. How interesting to find such old charities still surviving and effectively operating after having been adapted to up-to-date circumstances.

Cheselbourne

➤ Once upon a time, on the high downs of the county of Dorset, the Giants of Dorset made sport and amused themselves by throwing large boulders across this valley. They stood upon Nettlecombe Tout and some of their stones landed on a place now known as Henning (or Hanging) Hill. One of the Giants, in vexation at always losing, is said to have fretted and died. The Giants have long gone, but the

'Giants Grave' still remains, and legend has it that when the cocks crow in Cheselbourne, the stones upon it move.

Today the oldest surviving building is the flint-built and once thatched chapel at Lyscombe, a resting place for monks and holy travellers halfway between the two important establishments of Milton Abbey and Cerne Abbas. Sadly, the buildings are now badly delapidated, but there is evidence of their former importance.

In pre-Reformation times, Lyscombe hamlet was much larger, comprising between 13 to 20 houses, but that gradually decreased in number and today only the ruins of the chapel and barn remain. It is supposedly on the site of a Roman villa, and before being attached to the parish in 1882, Lyscombe belonged to Milton Abbey. Later it passed to a John Tregonwell, lord of the manor of Milton Abbas, who sold the hamlet and chapel to a yeoman named Miller in 1755. At some time the buildings were used as a bakehouse and loghouse.

The chapel is especially worthy of attention, measuring 40 ft in length and 17 ft wide. The main walls were two ft six inches thick and the windows were of Norman origin. Tradition says the chapel was dedicated to St Mary the Virgin.

The flint built parish church occupies a commanding position on the left as one approaches the village from the south. The site looks as if it has been levelled at some time and the structure of the tower gives it an appearance of height. The church is dedicated to St Martin. Son of a Roman soldier, he is best remembered for sharing his cloak with a beggar.

Interesting features include a 12th century stone font and, springing from a corbel in the western wall, a grotesque head wearing a double fool's cap. Also worthy of note are the Cheselbourne 'Boys', restored to the church in 1898 and now resting on the corbels in the north aisle. There are various slab monuments and plaques commemorating former rectors and their families and also a coat of arms of the Keyte family, who occupied the manor farm until 1623.

After the Middle Ages history seems to have passed Cheselbourne by. In 1348 the village was almost wiped out by the Black Death. Cheselbourne had at that time a population of nearly 1,000 and the disease reached them from the port of Melcombe Regis. A plague pit was discovered several years ago when the graves were being levelled in the churchyard. The victims shared a communal grave as few survived to dig individual resting places for their loved ones, and one wonders if perhaps the village remained deserted for a few decades until survivors returned to their homes and the land was considered safe from the ravages of the deadly disease.

There is a legend that still awes school children today – the tale of Ann Riggs, the local village witch. Many misfortunes were attributed to her powers. One farmer blamed her for the death of nine of his horses which she is supposed to have ridden to exhaustion during successive night rides.

Several times she was refused access to fields to gather sticks for firewood and the farmer concerned blamed her for the subsequent death of his cows.

Traditionally the local witch coven met in the holy road above withybeds to the north-west of the parish, towards Melcombe Bingham. These withybeds are still very boggy. A coachman and his horses taking the double bend at speed is reputed to have disappeared without trace into a watery grave one dark and stormy night.

But on this particular night, the witches were surprised by the local witch-hunter general and his henchmen and they were arrested and carted off to the nearest ducking stool, the local stream being too shallow.

During the melee that ensued, poor Ann Riggs was killed and was buried just outside the churchyard. However, in the years that followed, the villagers, ridden with guilt, decided to give Ann a proper Christian burial. They even extended the walls of the churchyard to include her in the consecrated ground and gave her a proper inscribed gravestone, which survives to this day.

She is supposed to have lived in a shack behind the cottage opposite the church, which became known as Carriers Cottage, and until recently served as a village shop and post office. During renovations of the cottage and garden some tunnels were revealed indicating possible storage of ice blocks or cheeses. A recent occupant of the cottage, during more renovations, discovered a peculiar stone with strange mystical symbols, pointing to the connections of Ann Riggs with the occult. It is also claimed that the cottage is haunted.

Descendants of the Rigg family still inhabit the village. Research into the parish registers reveal Riggs mentioned in records as early as 1644, but whether the family or the headstone really relate to the witch is hard to say.

Child Okeford

The village of Child Okeford is tucked beneath the great ridge of Hambledon Hill, the site of a Neolithic long barrow and an impressive hill fort covering some 31 acres. It is said that General Wolfe used the hill as a training ground for his men, prior to the storming of the Heights of Quebec in 1759.

The little church of St Nicholas has, displayed in a case near the pulpit, a copy of the so-called 'Bishops Bible' of 1568. The church also has some surprising musical connections. The first public performance of the music for *Onward Christian Soldiers*, by Sir Arthur Sullivan, was put on here. Another popular hymn, *All People That on Earth do Dwell*, was composed by Sir William Kethe, who was rector here from 1561 to 1608.

Christchurch

➤Well known to professional coastal fishermen and the coastal and dinghy sailing fraternity, but not always apparent to those on land, is the Run. Christchurch is built at the point where the rivers Stour and Avon run into the sea. It has been a port since well before the Norman Conquest, but never developed into a major harbour because of the problems posed by this dangerous piece of water.

The narrow stretch of tidal water is constrained to seaward by constantly moving sandbanks, and to landward by the Christchurch Haven quay. It is the gauntlet that every boat has to run when either departing from, or entering Christchurch harbour.

At few other places are the predicted times of low and high water, barometric pressure, wind speed and direction considered so assiduously. Even so, having got all the facts right does not guarantee an easy passage through the Run.

You may be privileged to see the Run in one of its annual periods of supreme physical glory. 'High water springs, together with abnormally low barometric pressure and a gale force eight, gusting ten from the south-west, combined to heap this enraged water mass, now powered with energy absorbed from the gale, into serrated columns of waves. Each one advancing over the sandbank, across the Run to the quay wall where, partly rebuffed, water cascaded over the quay whilst the greater majority of energy was transformed into waves which, reversing their direction, went surging back across the Run to meet and do battle with the next bank of water converging over the sandbank.

'Spume and spray, whipped from the foaming crests of these waves, formed a mist that, carried by the wind, engulfed trees, buildings and motor vehicles with its saltladen breath.

'The sea, now discoloured to a brownish hue by entrained sand stirred from the seabed, swirled to seaward some 200 or

300 yards topped by a moving carpet of sprindrift fleeing from the wind: whilst the bay within the low visibility afforded was covered by creaming combers rushing shorewards.'

On other occasions the Run is a soft, gentle, mirror-smooth surface reflecting the moon, stars, and the red light of the Needles lighthouse from across the bay.

Of course, the very difficulties posed by the Run for shipping made Christchurch an ideal port for smugglers. For the whole of the 18th century and into the 19th, Christchurch was probably one of the busiest smuggling centres in the country. The gentle sandy beaches were ideal for landing cargoes, and the townsfolk became adept at evading the surveillance of the Revenue men. The two bridges into the town could easily be blocked by an 'accidentally' overturned cart or a milling flock of animals, so cutting off access from the landward side. There are many reminders of Christchurch's smuggling past still to be found in a walk around the town.

Dorchester

Hardly hidden, but often overlooked, is the bronze statue of Dorset's 'other' poet, William Barnes. It is impossible not to be aware of Thomas Hardy's importance when travelling about Dorset, but for people outside the county this has tended to overshadow the achievements of William Barnes, already 40 years old when Hardy was born.

Barnes loved his county as Hardy did, but he wrote gentler, dialect pieces, inspired by the beauty of the countryside and by the poignancy of human feelings.

He was born in the Vale of Blackmore, at Rushay on Bagber Heath, but when he was 18 he came to Dorchester to work for a firm of solicitors. It was here that he met the love of his life, Julia Miles. To show her father that he was a worthy suitor, he became a schoolmaster, and in 1827 they were married.

William opened his own school in Dorchester and his first poems were published in 1844. He and Julia were extremely happy and their family grew to include six children. Then tragedy struck with Julia's death in 1852. William never got over her loss. He took Holy Orders and was sent as curate to Whitcombe, just outside Dorchester. The church there is a memorial to the gentle poet. He was buried at Winterborne Cane nearby.

Also close to the heart of Dorchester folk was the Candlemas Fair. This was the day when Dorchester came to life – it was the day when all your friends and relations who lived in the country came to the county town to enjoy the fun of the fair. They came from all the surrounding villages, either by the carrier's cart or on foot.

The day started with the stalls being erected in the town. From the town pump to the Antelope Hotel the stalls sold all manner of home-made sweets, rock of various flavours and brandy snaps. This, of course, was a delight to the children because they could purchase their sweets before going to school, in case the stalls were sold out later!

In front of the County Museum the stalls selling lino and carpets were situated. Their busiest time was in the evening, when the stalls were lit with naptha flares, and husbands had finished work and were available to take their wives to choose a new piece of floor covering. The stall holders were kept busy until very late at night.

Outside the Corn Exchange, stalls were packed with clothes, and in North Square the cheap jacks sold their wares with the usual lines of persuasive patter and tricks of the trade, eg china which would not break however harshly treated.

In the Fairfield on Weymouth Avenue the horse dealers plied their trade, and many a horse changed ownership, but no money was offered at the time – just a slap of hands, obviously a gentlemen's agreement.

The main business was the hiring of workers. Any man wishing to change his employment carried the tools of his trade so that a prospective employer knew just what the man's trade was. If man and employer were compatible the agreement was that the man would take up his new post on Lady Day.

There was one good lady, Miss Daisy Whitehead, who kept a fruit store in South Street and looked very attractive dressed as one of the Criers of London and selling her wares to the cry of 'Violets, lady, sweet violets'.

About midnight the crowds would disperse, the stallholders would pack up and peace was restored to the County Town.

Edmondsham

On the green at Edmondsham, the village people have planted a tree and set up a plaque to show their appreciation of a local couple, Mr and Mrs Catterall. Mrs Catterall runs the little post office and general store, and was clerk to the parish council for many years. She and her husband are 'always there to help out' no matter what crisis arises. Here is the hidden heart of a Dorset village, seldom so publicly displayed.

Edmondsham can boast only some 160 inhabitants, but this little village, just over a mile from Cranborne, is beautifully kept and has a 12th century church and a late Elizabethan manor house.

Strolling past the imposing red brick houses with their tall facades bearing the inscription of their builder, 'H.M.' – Hector Munro, you come to the village pump. Now disused, this was the main watering place for the whole village in days gone by. A splendid edifice, built in 1884, this also has the 'H.M.' inscription on the stone plinth holding the unusually large galvanised tap. Behind this tap is the wrought iron wheel complete with chains which the villagers used to draw their water. The whole is sheltered under a canopy of strong oak beams, over which is a slate roof topped with a lead ball.

To the right of the pump is Keeper's Lane, so-called because at the end of this three quarter mile track lies the cottage of the keeper of Edmondsham Woods.

Edmondsham Woods are a sheer delight for nature lovers. Birds abound, especially in springtime when they fill the whole woodland with bird song. Often when one walks through the woods towards Cranborne, one will encounter a deer or two. These shy creatures occasionally emerge from their woodland haven to survey the world outside and if the walker is very quiet and gentle, they will sometimes stand and stare at you before bounding away into the thick brambles.

Ferndown

In the 18th century there was a great deal of smuggling activity and the Dorset coastline was a perfect venue for it, with its miles of beaches stretching from Weymouth to Hengistbury Head. Poole harbour was a favourite place for bringing in contraband, which was often hidden in the church at Kinson.

One of the most famous leaders of the smugglers was named Isaac Gulliver, and he and his band of smugglers would fetch the contraband from Kinson church to take it inland on the backs of ponies. They had a track across the moors from Kinson, down what is now the New Road from Bournemouth to Ferndown and from there joined a deep, sandy track between high banks, which is now the Golf Links Road at Ferndown. This track crossed over at Tricketts

51

Cross and went behind what is now the Coach House Motel, across the moors to West Moors and from there on through Fordingbridge to Salisbury. One day on this route, they met a body of Excise men in Fordingbridge, who had come down the road from Southampton. They had a pitched battle, and, the story went, 'The yard of the George Hotel ran red with blood!'

How strange it is, that the Ferndown Golf Links Road, with its lovely gardens and pretty houses was once a smugglers track. I wonder if anyone has ever woken in the night and heard the wind in the trees and the rustling of the branches and thought it was the sound of soft Dorset voices whispering and the trotting of ponies!

The Fleet

The Chesil Bank was laid down by the sea, long before the last Ice Age. It is some 18 miles long, stretching from Portland to Burton Bradstock, and over the centuries has become notorious for shipwrecks.

The stones are said to be so graded that a fisherman of those parts can tell where he is at night, by the size of the stones he treads on.

Behind the Chesil is a stretch of brackish water, forming a lagoon some 200 yards wide, known as the Fleet.

For hundreds of years, this water has been the home of swans, eaten by the monks of Abbotsbury when food was scarce in the winter. When they were counted in the reign of Elizabeth I, they numbered some 850 birds, today the count is approximately the same.

In the 17th century some Dorset men tried to drain the Fleet, to make agricultural land. The scheme was not a success as 'men had to wear boards on their feet, in order to walk, because of the mud'.

The sculptor Epstein used a sketch of the underside of an

Abbotsbury swan's wing for his bronze of St Michael trampling on the devil in Coventry Cathedral, when it was rebuilt after the Second World War.

Another wartime association is with Barnes Wallace, inventor of the bouncing bomb. This amazing invention was tried out on the Fleet, without an explosive charge, before it went into production. For years this bomb lay on the edge of the water gathering a coat of green weeds, then a few years ago the authorities gave it to the Fleet Air Arm Museum at Yeovilton.

Fordington

Life in Dorset, and elsewhere, has changed beyond all recognition during the 20th century. Yet the past still lives in the memories of local people. Take Fordington in about 1905, for instance.

'Fordington at this time was just a small village. It had its farms – Mr Churchill's on the Green and Oddy's in St George's Road. The cows would meander down the hill to The Cross along Kings Road to Oddy Mead, which was later given as a playing field to the children of the village. The cows returned slowly at 4 pm for milking as if they knew the time of day.

'There were bakehouses in Holloway Road and Culliford Road and another on the corner of St George's Road. After the bread was baked housewives took along the Sunday joint to be cooked. The bread was made from corn grown on the farms of Dorset and ground at the roller mill at the bottom of Mill Street. The noise of the water wheel was deafening.

'Three laundries, which served all the area, were in Mill Street, Wareham Road and St George's Road, all run by women and everything done by hand. Wages were five shillings a week, hours long and work hard, but everything was spotlessly white.

'A blacksmith and a wheelwright served the community, also a boot and shoe repairer although in most cases the husband would repair the family boots and shoes. There was a grocer's shop on The Green, a sweet shop in Holloway Road and another in Mill Street. A lot of sweets could be bought for one penny!

'Mill Street was known as 'the land of children', there were so many. They played safely in the stream and fields. Most people were poor and the only help, if they were lucky, was the parish relief and one cwt of coal and a round of beef at Christmas.

'St George's Church school had as its headmistress a Miss Kimber, who was greatly loved by all her pupils. There was no milk or school dinners and many of the children went hungry, but some parents when they could spare it gave their children a little extra to share with the others.

'All babies were born at home and delivered by the two midwives, Mrs Rocket and Granny Cox. The mother was bound with a binder and always breast-fed her baby. The mother was kept in bed for ten days and for some reason it was considered unlucky to get up on the ninth day. She had to be 'churched' before meeting anyone outside her immediate family. Families were large and mother would push the pram with the new baby at the top end, a little one about 14 months old at the other end and two toddlers holding the handle at both sides. Life was hard for the womenfolk.

'The main meal of the day was stew and would cost about 4d, 2d for the meat and 2d for vegetables, and suet pudding to fill the gaps in an empty stomach. Bread and jam was the food for the rest of the day.

'The average age for a girl to marry was 18 and soon had a cottage to rent at four shillings a week. Water came from the wells and one open toilet served four cottages. Sewerage was put in about 1920, the same time as tap water.

'Everything was delivered by horse and cart. Milk was delivered early in the day by a very pretty float shining with polished brass. You took your own jug and the milk came straight from the churn – one dipper full and a little bit extra, and a chat about which cow had gone dry, Bluebell or Daisy, and who had had a baby up the road.

'Everyone went 'sticking' to provide fuel for the open fires, blackberrying and mushrooming in the seasons.

'All children went to Sunday school, not so much for religious instruction as to give parents a little time to themselves. The only outing was the Sunday school trip to Weymouth once a year. Some people never left the village, not even to go as far as Dorchester.

'If you were a young married woman you would wake at 6 am and feed your baby, who would be in bed with you all night – there were no cots then. There was no need to look out of the window to check on the weather, you would know. The bedroom would be icy cold with frost on the windows in winter, and the lino-covered floor freezing to the feet. You would hear your husband downstairs raking out the ashes to light a fire to boil the kettle for that first cup of tea. You would put your baby back in the bed between the pillows, light your candle and find your way downstairs to start work and get the other children up. All water had to be heated on the kitchen fire and all cooking was done on this same fire.

'Times were hard but, with hindsight, everyone seemed happy and all the summers seemed to be filled with endless sunshine.'

Frampton

Frampton lies six miles north-west of Dorchester on the A356. Until 1931 it was mainly an estate village with most of the property, whether farmhouse or cottage, owned by one family, the Sheridans, who were related descendants of Richard Brinsley Sheridan the poet. Prior to their incumbency, the squires of the parish were the Brownes, and between them, they altered and improved the character of Frampton.

Because of the geography of the parish, with the river Frome running through its entire length, it is very much a

Wren's Bridge, Frampton

village of bridges, there being five in all. Two are farm bridges connecting fields on either side of the river, but the other two are road bridges and the fifth is a viaduct.

The two road bridges were built by Squire Browne in about 1790, at the time he enlarged the family house to a

grand 40 bedroom mansion. They are both constructed in the classical style, one from a design by Sir Christopher Wren and known locally as 'Wren's Bridge'. This bridge with its curving graceful lines and fine palladian-style balustrading of Portland stone has three arches. When Squire Browne was told that the river was not wide enough to accommodate three spans, he is said to have retorted 'Then widen it!', so determined was he to have an impressive approach to his enlarged country seat!

The second of the Squire's fine bridges can be found on the road to Southover. Again three-arched in classical style and brick built, but instead of the stone balustrade there is an attractive timber parapet constructed in the Japanese style and painted white. There used to be a smaller version, a footbridge about 100 yards down river for the benefit of the family and their servants, to gain quick access to the church and village, but sadly after years of neglect it finally succumbed to a flood in the 1970s. The road bridge is known locally as Sandways Bridge, so called because it was built over a sandy bottomed stretch of the river where there was once a ford. This is a very popular spot with villagers as a place to meet or just 'to stand and stare'. Many a hopeful small boy has dangled his makeshift line from this bridge, keeping a weather eye open for the water bailiff as he does so. You might even be rewarded by a fleeting glimpse of a kingfisher skimming along the river.

The last bridge, is on the parish boundary with Grimstone, on the Dorchester–Yeovil road. It is a magnificent viaduct, built in handcut Portland stone under the direction of no less a person than Isambard Kingdom Brunel, the great Victorian engineer, in 1857 to take the railway across the river Sydling and the road. As the Great Western Railway had formed an excellent working relationship with the Sheridans, over whose land they were laying the line, the company agreed to build a tunnel so that the trains wouldn't be seen from the house and also a small 'halt' at Grimstone. Trains would stop there, it was agreed, just as long as there was a Sheridan living in Frampton. All of which would appear to be a most civilized way of making 'progress'!

Of all the hundreds of motorists who pass by each day, how many actually notice this splendid example of the great engineer's work. Frampton is fortunate indeed to have had two internationally famous designers from different eras leave their mark on the landscape.

Today, few of us would stop to ponder the question 'In the past, how did the big houses keep their vast supply of rich and exotic foods fresh?' The answer is an icehouse.

The icehouse would have been built in the garden in a shady position with the door facing north. The owner would have had the choice of two types of construction, the icehouse, which was built entirely above ground and the icewell, which was set partly or totally below ground.

The type that was built at Frampton Court, most probably by Squire Browne, is in fact a partly sunken icewell. A sphere or inverted cone was proved to be the most efficient shape for the interior of the store and Frampton's is of the latter design. It is built of brick which has aged most attractively, it's beehive-shaped roof being adorned with lichens, wild flowers and ivy. It has two entrances, the main one beautifully arched, where there would have been two doors, one inside the other to form an airlock. The other is a smaller side entrance raised on a bank for filling the well with the ice.

The collection and storing of the ice was the responsibility of the head gardener. It would have been cut into large blocks and carried on a farm wagon to its destination. If it was being stored in an icewell, the blocks were broken into small pieces, and straw packed at the base, sides and top for added insulation and drainage of the melted ice. Some houses had special icepools, but many just used stagnant ponds and ditches, which sounds quite disgusting, particularly as they often laid food on the ice to keep it fresh, used it in iced drinks, for making ice cream and for medicinal purposes!

The ice that was used in the Frampton icehouse was obtained from a pond only a few yards away, alleged to have been constructed by Benedictine monks, who lived there in earlier times. It is to be hoped that the ducks and other waterfowl did not have access!

Around 1815, the winters began to get warmer and soon it was not possible to collect ice from local sources. Some canny merchant conceived the idea of importing ice from Norway and this proved so successful that Norwegian schooners were soon ploughing the waves of the North Sea to many British ports with their icy cargos. Frampton's supply would have come from Weymouth, where there was a large ice store on the quay. The eventual demise of the icehouse came in the 1860s when the forerunner of the refrigerator was invented.

The well of the Frampton icehouse has now been filled in and it is used as a toolshed but if you walk inside even now, the interior is quite chilly. It is well worth a visit, the curved walls and roof inside are in excellent condition and the perfect symmetry of the construction is remarkable.

You will find it at the Court at Southover which is now a fruit and dairy farm owned and run by Mr and Mrs Lazenby and Mr and Mrs Stephens, who are always pleased to show this curiosity of a bygone age to anyone who is interested.

Another hidden 'house' of quite a different sort is a much neglected part of the history of the Second World War, namely the pillbox!

In 1940, when Britain had her back to the wall after the fall of Dunkirk, a major operation was very rapidly set in motion by the government, to defend our islands in the event of a German invasion. During the summer of that year, many thousands of pillboxes were hastily erected to accommodate troops with machine guns and rifles should such as appalling occurence arise.

Dorset being a southern coastal county was very much in the front line, and as well as the actual coastline being heavily defended, the hinterland was also fortified as the next line of defence should the enemy break through. Chosen lines of defence were river valleys, railway lines and other geographical weak spots.

Frampton fell into the river valley *and* railway line category and was therefore an obvious choice for fortification. In fact, there was a line of pillboxes built from Wareham at the mouth of the river Frome to Maiden Newton near its source.

Of the twelve or so built in the parish, two remain on the railway line and three in a water meadow. The latter can be found near the south entrance to the village.

There were numerous designs, mostly of concrete and constructed by local builders under the watchful eye of the Royal Engineers from designs made by the rather grandly named 'Fortifications and Works at the War Office'! Frampton's pillboxes, however, were constructed from brick which has mellowed over 50 years and now plays host to an abundance of flora and fauna as well. They certainly are very snug inside. What better place to hibernate!

The pillboxes are hexagonal in shape, set partly below ground with steps down. Each has six or eight small windows called loops for observation. The walls are one foot in width and there is a foot of concrete on the roof.

It is doubtful whether the Frampton pillboxes would have withstood very heavy bombardment, but their role was to 'hold' the enemy until mobile units could be moved in to take the strain. However, they were only used once as battle stations in September 1940, at the time of an expected German invasion code-named 'Sealion', and were never put to the test. A local inhabitant, who lived in the village during the war, relates that they were sometimes used for Home Guard practice. There are those who are of the opinion that their construction throughout the country was, in fact, a psychological exercise to reassure the population! But a few still stand, whatever their intended use; a memorial to the invasion that thankfully never took place.

One of these three can be found on the bridleway through the wrought iron gates at the south entrance to the village about 100 yards from the main road. The other two are in the field directly on the left, but can just as easily be reached from the main road itself, through a strip of woodland. Each forms the point of a triangle about 150 yards apart, strategically placed across the valley. It would be courteous to ask permission of the owner at Littlewood Farm before walking through the meadows.

Gillingham

▬ Among the lush pastures of the spacious Blackmore Vale in North Dorset lies the historic town of Gillingham. Though fairly modern in appearance, its origins go back to early Saxon days. In medieval times Norman kings built a hunting lodge here, later called a palace.

All that now remains of the former royal lodge or palace are grass-covered mounds at the end of Kingscourt Road, off the Shaftesbury road on the outskirts of Gillingham.

It is not known precisely when it was built but Henry I visited the lodge in 1132 and Henry II was a regular visitor. There are also records of visits by King John and his son, Henry III.

Eventually the palace, as it became known, fell into disrepair, so Edward III in 1369 ordered that it should be demolished. Much of the material was removed to repair other royal residences in the south. About 1399 Henry IV ordered that what remained should be dug up.

To gather the best flavour of Gillingham's history, a visit can be paid to the town's small museum in a pair of 17th century cottages in Church Walk, close to St Mary's parish church, and to the church itself.

In the museum is evidence that, even before Gillingham became a Saxon village, Romans or Romano-British lived in the area. There are finds, including a skeleton, from excavations made a few miles away at Todber, plus more recent discoveries of pottery sections and coins in Commonmead Lane, Gillingham. Here in 1974 housing development revealed the foundations of a fairly large Roman house with outbuildings.

The museum also contains a variety of articles manufactured, used or found locally and documents from the 13th century relating to the manor courts, to what was at one time the Royal Forest of Gillingham and to town life through the centuries until recent times.

Specific items are concerned with John Constable's association with the town – his painting of Gillingham town bridge over the river Shreen is in the Tate Gallery, and with Gillingham Fire Service (including a 200 year old fire engine).

A short distance from the museum is the old town lock-up, built around 1750 and used until the new police station was erected in 1880. Recently restored, it is used as an overflow store for the museum.

In the parish church the oldest archaeological object is an Anglo-Saxon cross shaft (AD 800–900) at the west end of the south aisle, still bearing its complicated interlaced pattern. Found embedded in the wall of the old vicarage (now Rawson Court, converted to an elderly people's home not far away), the shaft was removed to the church for safe-keeping.

It is thought to have been part of a standing cross and used either to mark a grave or as the centre of a sort of open air preaching spot. It was in use when King Alfred fought against the Danish invasions. Only four miles away up the hill at Shaftesbury he had founded a famous nunnery.

The most historic part of the church building is the chancel (1270–1370). Its five great pointed windows, with their trefoil heads, on the south side of the chancel indicate that it was built in the Decorated Gothic style which was popular in the 14th century.

In those days the chancel was used only by the priests. While the Creed and Gloria were being sung, the priest and his assistants sat in the three seats which still remain on the south wall. They had their own door, which can still be seen on the south side below the third window.

The chancel was added to a much older church dating back to Norman or even Saxon times. Almost all other traces of this building were destroyed when it was demolished in 1838 and when most of the present church was built. It is probable that the chancel roof was made from wood from the Royal Forest of Gillingham.

On either side of the central aisle of the church are the bench ends, which must have been part of the 15th century church. They are carved in the Perpendicular Gothic style. Also constructed in the same style are the font at the far west end of the church under the tower and a richly carved rood screen (1547–1553) at the east end of the north aisle.

The screen had separated the ordinary people from the chancel, which was then St Catherine's chantry chapel, where masses were said for the souls of the family which had founded it. After the Reformation the chantry chapel was closed. Now the remains of the screen stand in front of the former chapel, which itself has become a choir vestry.

The Grove (Portland)

St Peter's church in the Grove at Portland is unique. The stone-built Romanesque edifice in the middle of what was formerly the island prison complex, was built and furbished by convicts during the reign of Queen Victoria.

When one remembers that these convicts were some of the worst in the country, it is hard to visualise them, in their prison clothing stamped with distinctive arrows, carefully and with great precision fashioning the walls and roof of this prison church in the 1870s; or to imagine the work and craftsmanship that went into creating and carving a fine pulpit and matching lectern out of solid blocks of Portland stone. The litany desk was added somewhat later by convict C. W. Brown, who was an artist in woodcraft.

Consecrated in 1872, it is rather unfortunate that not all the names of the convicts responsible for this unique church were recorded. However, it is known that the mosaic pavement in the sanctuary, an intricate repeated pattern in black and white, based on a pavement in Rome, was created by Constance Kent.

In the late 1860s, Constance Kent had been found guilty of the murder of her four year old half-brother five years previously and sentenced to hang. However within a fortnight the sentence was commuted to penal servitude for life and she was sent to Portland prison.

After serving 20 years she was released, still only aged 41. All trace of her was lost but her legacy remains for those who wish to see.

Halstock

◄ The pub in Halstock is called the Quiet Woman, and the inn sign shows a woman carrying her severed head under her arm. This is not just a masculine jibe at women's alleged talkativeness, but refers to the legend of St Juthware. St Juthware or Judith is said to have lived in Halstock, and met her martyrdom on a hill near the village, where a field still carries her name.

She is thought to have lived in the 7th or 8th century, and to have been of Celtic origin and not Saxon. She was of noble birth, and from an early age devoted herself to serving God and performing good works, in particular attending to the needs of visiting pilgrims. She had three sisters, Sidwella,

Edwara and Wilgitha (who were also destined to become saints) and a brother called Bana, a man easily aroused to anger. After her mother's death her father remarried, and the new stepmother was jealous of Juthware's piety and sought to cause trouble. Her opportunity came after Juthware's father died.

Juthware, who looked pale and ill, as a result of much fasting and keeping vigil, complained of pains in her chest. Her stepmother, with the appearance of maternal affection, advised her to apply freshly made cheese to her chest before going to church, assuring her that it would ease the pain. Meanwhile the stepmother lied to Bana that Juthware was with child. When they came out of church, Bana accused Juthware of being pregnant, and finding her undergarments wet with milk, flew into a rage. Notwithstanding her denials, he struck off her head with his sword. She then picked up her head from the ground, walked into the church and placed it on the altar, watched in wonder by the gathered assembly.

A holy spring appeared in the place where her head had lain, and many miracles later took place at her tomb. Her relics were eventually taken to Sherborne Abbey in the 10th century, and she was greatly venerated there.

Local legend says that her ghost may be seen in the lane on the hill where she died, but no sightings have been recorded lately, and when the Rev J. Slater, then rector of this parish, went ghost-hunting, it must be admitted that she failed to appear.

One of Halstock's hidden claims to fame is the unusual naming of some of the fields. Where else do you find a Cassius, Brutus or Messala, a Toleration, Constitution or Education, or even a Massachusetts or a Boston?

These names were given to the fields by Thomas Hollis of Essex, who purchased a large estate in Halstock and Corscombe in 1741. Hollis was an eccentric character, said by some to be an atheist, with political views much suspected by the establishment. He was also a philanthropist and scholar, who detested corruption and tyranny in all its forms. He made many benefactions to university libraries, and in particular to that of Harvard University in America. Holliston in the USA is named after him, and there is a Hollis Hall at Harvard University.

He spent the last few years of his life on his estate in Dorset. He died in 1774, and the story is told that when he died, on his farm in Corscombe, he was buried at his own wish, ten ft deep in one of his own fields. His grave was immediately ploughed over so that no trace of it remained.

His legacy to Corscombe and Halstock was his renaming of the farms and fields which he had bought. He called them by the names of the champions of Liberty for the most part, this being interpreted as anyone who had helped to free the human spirit. Neville, Locke, Sydney and Marvell Farms are named after authors he approved of, Harvard Farm after the university with which he had such strong links, and Liberty Farm is self-explanatory.

To rename the farms would have been enough for most people, but Hollis was not content until he had renamed all the fields as well. Some were called after patriots and heroes whom he venerated, some after abstract virtues, some after American states. At Locke Farm, for instance, the fields are named – Molineux, Hollis, Limburg, Baron Coste, Hutchinson, Masham, Christchurch, Lay-preacher, Education, Constitution, Government, Toleration, Holland, Oxford, Understanding, Reasonableness, Comprehension, and Nassau.

There was even a Stuart Coppice. Why? The answer is that the hazel trees had to be beheaded often!

Most of the field names are still in use today. If Hollis left no tombstone, he certainly has a living memorial.

Halstock stands astride the Harrow Way, one of the oldest roads in Britain. It crossed the country from east to west, and, after reaching Yeovil, goes via Halstock and Corscombe to Beaminster Down, where it meets the other major Neolithic road, the Great Ridgeway. It then continues to the mouth of the Axe, its terminus.

Its path through the village has been obliterated by modern roads, but it emerges the other side as Common Lane, and may be followed as such to Corscombe. At the Halstock end there was a slight deviation in medieval times, and it is across this short stretch that the site of the Roman villa lies. (The prehistoric trackway would have run alongside it.) This Romano-British site has been excavated over a period of years, though nothing is now visible, as the site was backfilled after each season.

An Iron Age farmstead preceded the villa. It was developed and Romanized over a period of about 400 years. At the height of its economic development the villa site covered an area of one and a half hectares, with two winged-corridor type houses, extensive farm buildings etc. It was clearly the centre of a large estate. A splendid bath suite was included, which, in the final stage AD 340–350, consisted of a hot bath complex, a cold plunge bath or small swimming pool, a large unheated room with a highly decorative geometric design mosaic, and a room with a channelled hypocaust with a similar mosaic floor. This is a large bath suite of much greater sophistication than anything else on the site, and it poses some interesting questions. The detailed report of the excavation is awaited with keen anticipation!

Lastly, there is a tombstone in the churchyard to John Pitt, aged 102, whose life spanned three centuries. He was born on 26th January, 1799 and died on 20th January, 1901. The tombstone was erected by public subscription.

Higher Bockhampton

Thorncombe Wood at Higher Bockhampton, lying close to Thomas Hardy's cottage, is a popular spot for those who pass this way.

The wood, which lies on the western edge of Hardy's Egdon Heath, covers 45 acres and has been developed by the Dorset County Council and the Dorset Naturalist Trust as a sanctuary for wild life. Two walks are sign-posted but little winding paths tempt the adventurous to explore further.

A large pond at the top of a rather steep incline is home to many types of dragonfly which hover and dart over the water. At certain times of the year grass snakes can be seen swimming to and fro between the banks of the pond and a small island in the middle, on the look-out for frogs and other food. A small gate in the nearby fence is a reminder that the badger also roams here.

Many of the magnificent trees will remember the time when they provided cover for smugglers on their way inland from the coast and the many dark deeds that must have been enacted there. The Romans, too, knew Thorncombe Wood, as their road connecting Durnovaria (Dorchester) to Londinium (London) passed through there.

Rumour has it that the ghost of a Roman Centurion still patrols this ancient road – you have been warned!

Hinton St Mary

In the early 1960s an exciting discovery was made at Hinton St Mary, when the excavation of a Roman villa revealed what the British Museum has described as 'one of the most outstanding Christian remains from Roman Britain'. A mosaic floor, measuring over 26 ft by 17 ft, was found to include the earliest known mosaic representation of

Christ. It was carefully lifted from the site and is now at the British Museum.

The mosaic dated from the first half of the 4th century, and the villa it graced was probably the heart of a large country estate. Perhaps the wealthy occupants ran sheep on Cranborne Chase, or raised cattle and grew crops in the Blackmore Vale. What is certain is that this little settlement has been in existence in some form for at least 1,600 years.

The villa was found about a quarter of a mile from the church, on the west side of the B3092. St Peter's is an attractive church with a 15th century tower. It was largely rebuilt in 1846, but it does still possess a 12th century font. Next door to the church is the manor house, once the home of the Freke family. William Freke was an odd soul who gained notoriety in his own day by writing pamphlets on such subjects as dreams and visions and the New Jerusalem. Once he went too far and disagreed with the doctrine of the Trinity. Luckily for him, it was only his booklet that suffered at the hands of the public hangman, when it was publicly burned. He died in 1744, having convinced himself that he was a true prophet.

Holwell

The church of St Laurence is to be found by the tranquil Caundle brook, which marks the northern boundary of the parish. There is a reference in 1249 to the rector of Bishops Caundle poaching the King's deer in the company of William, the son of the vicar of Holwell! In 1301 Galfrid de Poleham became the first recorded rector.

Built in rather unusual order, the oldest part is the tower which dates from about 1470. The nave and north aisle and south or Brett Chapel were added circa 1480–86. In the 15th century there was a chancel but by 1770 it was replaced by a mean little structure, of which an interior picture is preserved in the county archives. In 1886 this was replaced by the present chancel which in turn was slightly improved in 1972 when the church was again refurbished.

The south chapel is the chantry founded by the Bishop of Abbotsbury for the prayers for the repose of the souls of Robert le Brett and his family. Robert le Brett was the King's Verderer in the ancient forest where this church stands, and it is because it was forest that the church is apparently detached from the rest of the village. Really it is not. The church would have been in one little clearing and the various settlements in others – Buckshaw, Sandhills, Foster's Hill and so on. Each little settlement was connected to the church and to each other by tracks.

There is a fine 15th century ceiling in the north aisle and traces of medieval painting on the pillars and a rood loft stairway. No trace of the rood loft remains, but there is a piece of wood from the gallery that was in the back of the church in the 18th and 19th centuries.

The church was extensively restored in 1885, when, sadly, the original frescoes were whitewashed. Some, apparently, were very frightening, depicting the Devil running after small boys with a pitchfork.

Carved in the lead roofing of the church tower are the initials of French prisoners from the Napoleonic Wars.

The old hour-glass was stolen a few years ago but old inhabitants remember being told by their fathers that when they were small their eyes were riveted on the sand running through, knowing that the hour would be up when there was none left and the sermon would end – only to be disappointed to see the rector turn it over on the iron bracket above the pulpit and go on preaching for another hour!

There are several ancient houses in the village. The oldest is Naish Farm which dates back to the 15th century. It is a fine example of a yeoman farmer's house with its thatched roof and its large chimney effectively dividing the rooms upstairs so that no partitions were necessary. There is a large inglenook fireplace downstairs and the original stone flags everywhere.

Little Westrow is another house of the same period. The original oak beams are in every room. One of the unusual features of the house is the stone fireplace with Tudor markings in one of the bedrooms. In the east wall outside there is a large bee-bole. In olden days these recesses were made to house a straw kep for bees. They nearly always faced east, the idea being that the rising sun woke the bees early for work, and so they produced more honey.

Woodbridge Farm is a very old thatched dwelling, built in the shape of a cross, although the back is the only original part left. This was known as the monastery schoolroom. Attics over the cheeseroom, which were panelled, were in cubicles and formed the dormitory. During excavations, several prayer books and sermons were found but were put back and a new floor nailed over them. It was almost surrounded by a deep dyke.

Although not of great antiquity, in the village stands the only Victorian post-box still in use. An entry in the Guinness Book of Records confirms this.

The manor is an imposing residence. Originally a farmhouse, it was supposedly one of King John's hunting lodges and was surrounded by a moat. In 1890 it was almost completely rebuilt and another storey added by an eccentric old man who had most of the moat filled in. He was afraid his pretty young wife would fall into it and drown. There was also an oubliette – a secret dungeon entered only by a trap-door in its ceiling. Here, again, it was filled in in case of disaster.

Legend has it that there was an underground passage running from the farm at Sandhills, which is on the old smuggling road from Bridport to the north, to the manor. This is probably quite true, as early this century a secret passage was found during the rebuilding of part of the farm. When the farmer lit a candle and went down the steps and

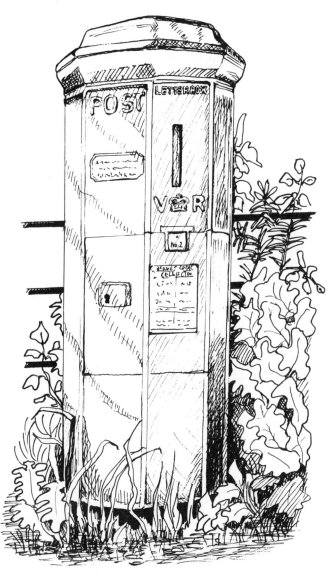

Holwell's Victorian post-box

into the tunnel, the light went out. 'Poisonous gas,' he muttered and had it blocked and built over. The old groom living at the manor at that time knew the whereabouts of a tunnel there, but had been sworn to secrecy by his father, so the secret died with him. It is interesting to note that the field in direct line between these two points is called 'Witches'. Evidently odd noises were heard from underground at times which led to its name. The present house has been much altered but still bears marks of great antiquity both inside and out.

At the beginning of the 20th century, the owner of one of the larger woods still kept a broom or besom tied to the top of the tallest tree to keep the witches away. Every few years a boy climbed up to renew it, for, as long as it was there no harm would befall anything in the woods. After a violent thunderstorm, he was very upset to find one of the beautiful silver firs had been struck by lightning and badly damaged. Puzzled that such a thing should happen, he went to look at the broom. It was no longer there and although he searched for several days no trace of it was ever found.

About the same time he came across an ash sapling which had been very expertly split through the middle for a distance of about 18 inches to two ft. He remembered his father telling him that if a new-born baby was in danger of dying, the only hope was to take it to haunted woods at dead of night, split a sapling and pass the baby through it. If it was done with the maximum of skill and the tree lived, then so would the baby. He decided to make a note of all the new-born babies in the village around that time. There were four of them. Each year he quietly noted the children's progress and that of the tree which in spite of the split, flourished. After twelve years he was saddened to hear that one little girl had contracted tuberculosis. He examined the tree. Was it his imagination or was it looking a bit unhealthy? The child died at the age of 13 and the little ash sampling died the same year.

Many old-fashioned remedies are still practised, such as keeping a large cob-web handy in an old out-house to place over a cut or wound to stop the bleeding. Up until 20 or so years ago, the oldest inhabitant always wore a snake skin stitched round the inside of his hat to prevent headaches. In his garden he kept a large bramble like a hoop, rooted at both ends, as his wife was prone to styes. If she crawled under the bramble three times against the sun, the stye would be cured quickly. When she got too old to stoop, she rubbed it with her wedding ring, which was almost as beneficial!

On the old turnpike road on the north-eastern boundary, which in the old days was notorious for footpads, lies a very gloomy pond known as Shovell's Pit, named after Admiral Sir Cloudisley Shovell's nephew. The Admiral was sailing in the *Association*, the flagship of the fleet in 1707, when it foundered at night on the rocks off the Isles of Scilly. When, early next morning, still alive, he was washed up, he was murdered by a woman for the sake of the ring he was wearing. His nephew, and heir, also in the Navy, set out on horseback to ride down to Devon, but he disappeared between Blandford and Sherborne. According to legend, he was robbed and murdered and his body thrown into this pond – hence the name. Within living memory, when Shovell's Pit was being dug out, part of a blue uniform with silver naval buttons appropriate to the date were found.

Kingston Lacy

➤ The estate of Kingston Lacy was bequeathed to the National Trust by Ralph Bankes in 1981.

The house and gardens are visited by thousands of people each year, but few visit the church of St Stephen situated at the edge of the park, built early this century. Above the porch is a statue of St Stephen patting a little boy, dressed in

Victorian clothes, on the head. The boy is Ralph Bankes, later owner of the estate.

Inside the church are several stained glass windows, one of which shows the Virgin and Child. Again, this is a protrait of Ralph, with his mother Henrietta as the Virgin Mary.

Less than a quarter of a mile to the south is a Saxon road, running from Winchester to Wareham, in those days a very important port. The road is called All Fools Lane, originally All Souls Lane, and it crosses the old Roman road which leads to Badbury Rings from Hamworthy.

There in a thick coppice, lie the humps and bumps of a Saxon village, together with a bank some three ft high, enclosing a rectangle, once the Saxon palace of King Ine (AD 688–726) owner of the original Kingston.

Lower Parkstone

St Peter's church was originally intended to have a spire over 200 ft in height, but unfortunately it was never built. It is a large church, which replaced the old chapel that was built in the early 19th century.

It was here that Lord Baden Powell and Miss Olave Soames, who lived at 'Grey Rig' in Lilliput, were married. Their eldest child was also christened here.

Baden Powell, who had found fame defending Mafeking in the Boer War, founded the Boy Scout movement not far from here, on the lovely island of Brownsea at the mouth of Poole harbour. Two years later, in 1910, so popular had the idea become with children, he and his sister Agnes founded the Girl Guides.

St Peter's church still has Scouts, Guides, Cubs and Brownies, and there is one local troop of Scouts who to this day are known as 'Lady Baden Powell's Own'.

Lyme Bay

The South West Peninsular Coast Path, 515 miles stretching from the Isle of Purbeck to Minehead, passes through Charmouth. Walking westwards up the cliffside path from the Charmouth Heritage Coast Centre brings you to a grassy plateau just before the coast path turns inland from the cliffs. Turning round and facing to the east, you can enjoy a spectacular panoramic view over Charmouth towards the distant horizons. For as far as the eye can see, this part of West Dorset is a designated Area of Outstanding Natural Beauty.

Out across Lyme Bay can be seen the Isle of Portland, with the lighthouse on Portland Bill at its extremity. Since the 17th century, from its extensive limestone quarries, Portland has provided stone for so many important buildings in London and other large cities. On the low, slender isthmus joining Portland with the mainland are the naval cranes and derricks of Portland Harbour. From this point westwards in the direction of Charmouth, along the foot of the coastal cliffs, is the beautiful sweep of Chesil Beach – a continuous 18 mile pebble bank unrivalled anywhere in the world. The most conspicuous of the cliffs, just three miles from this view-point, is Golden Cap. Rising to 191 metres (627 ft) above sea level, with the woods of Langdon Hill behind, this is the highest point on the south coast of England. The upper part of the cliff face is of greensand which, over the years, has weathered to the striking golden brown colour which gave the cliff its name.

Inland from the cliff-edge is a rising sweep of greensward, often grazed by sheep and much of it owned by the National Trust. You are looking here at one of the most attractive stretches of the Dorset Heritage Coast. A narrow, sunken lane can be discerned winding its way down into Charmouth. This is Stonebarrow Lane, and it is part of the original Roman road from Dorchester to Exeter. In fact, until the Turnpike Road was constructed in 1754 along what is now the line of the A35 trunk road, Stonebarrow Lane was still the main road from Dorchester, through Charmouth, to Exeter.

Down below cluster the rooftops of the village of Charmouth, from which rises the square stone tower of St Andrew's church which is in the centre of the village's conservation area. The estuary of the river Char meanders gently to the sea, past the reed marsh that is a haven for various species of wildlife, and near the slate-roofed Heritage Coast Centre that was once a cement factory. A thousand years ago and more, the river was called the Cerne, and Charmouth itself was recorded as 'Cernemude' in the Domesday Book, the name meaning 'the settlement at the mouth of the Cerne'.

Tracing the line of the river back inland, you can see right up the Char valley between its shoulders of dipping, rolling meadows leading past the little community of Whitchurch Canonicorum. The fields have a delightful irregularity about them, bordered as they are by thick, ancient hedges and relieved here and there by clumps and coppices of broad-leafed trees. Further round, inland, the ground rises to the tiny settlement of Catherston Leweston, huddling round its imposing old manor house. On the skyline beyond is the wooded crest of Conegar Hill, where rabbits once were warrened for the provision of meat for the local countryfolk.

A little further to the left, over the village of Wootton Fitzpaine and the rich, rolling farmland of the Marshwood Vale, are the unmistakable scarp and dip slopes of Pilsdon Pen. On its commanding summit, which at 277 metres (909 ft) is the highest point in Dorset, are the ramparts and ditches of an Iron Age hill fort. This was constructed in about 200 BC by the Durotriges, the local Celtic tribe, who had constantly to defend their territories against the onslaughts of other neighbouring tribes. Closer to hand, just three miles away, can be seen the wooded prominence of Coney's Castle, the site of another Iron Age hill fort. Some believe that the name derives from the Anglo-Saxon 'Cyning' or 'Conig', meaning 'King', and suggest that the Wessex King Egbert used the old hill fort as a base from which to beat off the marauding Vikings who landed at Charmouth with 35 ships in AD 833. However, it is just as likely that this was another rabbit warren like Conegar Hill, and that its name was similarly derived.

From this viewpoint it would have been possible to observe many stirring chapters in the history of the ancient Kingdom of Wessex. The land has been fought over by warring tribes, by Romans and by invading Vikings and Saxons. The chalk uplands were grazed throughout the Middle Ages by great flocks of sheep, the numbers of which did not begin to diminish until a hundred years ago. The river valleys and lowlands, once densely wooded, were laboriously cleared by our forefathers centuries ago, and brought under cultivation, leaving woods, spinneys and hedgerows that remain today as homes for game and wildlife. This is indeed a viewpoint to stir the fertile imagination of an appreciative observer.

Lyme Regis

➤ St Michael's church is set on the steep hillside which overlooks the little harbour created by Lyme's famous Cobb wall. Erosion is gradually bringing it closer to the sea, as is so common along this shifting coastline. It is a fascinating church, incorporating the earlier Norman building, with many interesting memorials and windows.

Both inside the church and outside in the churchyard are memorials to Mary Anning, the daughter of a local carpenter, who died in 1847. Mary Anning's story is a remarkable one.

The continents as we know them now were formed by the deposition of progressive layers of minerals. Most originated in deep or shallow seas, some were washed down in river deltas, and others were wind-blown from desert areas. Dorset displays excellent examples of almost every kind of geological stratum laid down during the last 200 million years. The strata of particular interest are those of the Mesozoic Era, the earliest of which were laid down during the Jurassic period. Along the Dorset coastline, and especially between Lyme and Charmouth, weathering and cliff erosion are constantly exposing fresh deposits to be eagerly studied by geologists. It is this ever-changing exposure of fresh deposits that makes the area so exceptional.

The Jurassic strata were laid down 135–190 million years ago, in a series of alternating bands of clay, sandstones and limestones. Rainwater that percolates down through the upper, porous layers of sandstones and limestones meets a barrier of impervious clay, and is diverted out to the edge of the cliffs in a series of springs. From time to time, and especially after very heavy rains, these upper layers slide on the wet, slippery clay, often setting off an inexorable flow of hundreds of tons of dark, viscid mud down the cliff face onto the beach below. These 'mud slides' are amongst the largest to be found anywhere in Europe.

Ammonite fossils and shells at Lyme Regis

It was in one of them – 'Black Ven', between Charmouth and Lyme Regis – that in 1811 a young girl named Mary Anning discovered one of the very first fossils of an ichthyosaur. These reptiles were abundant in the warm Mesozoic seas, together with such other sea creatures as ammonites, belemnites, sea urchins, and various molluscs. Fossilised remains of all these are easy to find on the beaches, and are a great attraction to visitors. The ammonites are flat, spiral fossils, which may be as small as a fingernail or as large as a bicycle wheel. Some are so large and heavy that they cannot be carried off the beach!

Mary went on to make other important discoveries and became known around the world for her fossil hunting. Anyone who wanders the streets of Lyme today cannot fail to be aware of her influence on her home town. She is buried in St Michael's churchyard, on the north side.

Lesser known contemporaries of Mary Anning were the Philpot sisters, Mary, Margaret and Elizabeth. They shared her love of fossil-hunting, and from 1805 lived at what is now the Anchor Hotel, at the top of Silver Street. The Philpot Museum, of which the author John Fowles is honorary curator, preserves their name.

Mrs Eleanor Coade and her daughter, also Eleanor, lived here for a while too. Mrs Coade made her name after the death of her husband in 1770. She ran a business in Lambeth making a reconstituted stone known as Coade Stone. Their house on the corner of Cobb Street and Pound Street was decorated by them with ornaments made in Coade Stone – a lasting shop window for the firm's products. The statue of George III in Weymouth is also of Coade Stone.

Lyme was as popular a resort in that period as it is today. Jane Austen loved the little town and came here in 1803 and 1804. In Broad Street a plaque was erected to mark Pyne House, where she is thought to have stayed. Many of her fans still come to see where Louisa Musgrove fell from the steps of the Cobb in *Persuasion*.

Lytchett Matravers

➤ Long since deserted by its aristocratic landlords, the Maltravers, even until recent times Lytchett Matravers was comparatively isolated. Six miles from any town, its inhabitants engaged in farming, brick making and building and agricultural contracting, with steam engines based at a cottage appropriately called 'The Depot'.

All the old cottages face south-east with their backs to the prevailing westerlies, trapping the morning sun in their windows. Many still command a panoramic view of the whole of Purbeck and Poole Harbour, even to the open sea. It is only natural that such a community must have used this uninterrupted view to its advantage. Iron Age men watched from Bulbury camp as trading galleys from the Mediterranean entered the harbour and would set off to meet them at Hamworthy or Wareham. In the 18th century smugglers used the lonely roads to convey their contraband inland to the north and west.

Superstition flourished and the inevitable smuggling cover-up operations produced the usual crop of ghost stories involving coffin bearers late into the night and the headless horsemen. The apparition of a brightly lit hearse crossing the Huntick Road and sometimes the main A350 still persists to this day and is said to reveal itself at least once to every generation.

Out towards the west of the village is a trackway, which comes from the direction of Bulbury hill fort and leads eventually to Badbury Rings. As it passes by the Old Park it plunges into a very deep and wooded place, green, ferny and mysterious, leading steeply downhill. Most of the time water runs down the pathway and bubbles over the stones; only dry in the hottest of summers.

It is a public bridleway and footpath, but it has been a trackway for probably a thousand years or more. To walk down, alone, is to relive time through the centuries. One can imagine cloaked travellers, journeying long ago, hurrying anxiously so as not to be benighted and maybe worried by the deep gloom as tree branches clash overhead in winter storms. Or perhaps making their way leisurely, grateful for the cool shade in the summer, or for the shelter from the icy winds of the winter.

All that time the path has been trodden by the passage of many feet, bare and dusty, or maybe wrapped in cloth and leather strips, or shod in wooden pattens which must have made descent or ascent difficult. The feet of horses and oxen, iron shod, have worn the path, and the rims of cartwheels have cut the track ever deeper and deeper.

Flowers grow in profusion on the banks in springtime. Primroses in great, buttery clots attempt to crowd out the dainty daffodils and straggling violets. Tiny white wood anemones gently sway in the darker corners. Later in the season, green ferns are interspersed with clumps of pink campion, spears of foxgloves and white meadowsweet.

Birds sing and chatter continually, moving here and there and ahead as one intrudes into their leafy, secret places. Lizards sun themselves on the sandy banks when the tree canopy overhead gives way to form a clearing. Rabbits and deer, nibbling at the vegetation, are often surprised into flight; rabbit bob-tails flashing white, and graceful deer leaping, white rumps betraying retreat.

Blind Hollow is the local name for this secret place and it marks the boundary of the old deerpark pale. Was it already a deep and steep blind hollow in medieval days when the park pale was thrown up to keep the game in and the peasant out? Is it called Blind Hollow because it is impossible to see out into the deer park or to the meadows on the other side?

Recently a BP pipeline was entrenched across the southern end of the trackway, but fortunately it has only opened up the 30 or so yards where the hollow meets the road.

A field to the south of the manor house and the church in

Lytchett Matravers is reputed to be the site of the medieval village. This was a busy place in times gone past. Its secrets have been long hidden from all but those who search them out.

On the south-west side of the field is a copse which conceals a green lane. It seems that at one time the green lane led southwards but when the village was decimated by the Black Death in the mid 14th century, it was no longer used. For about 300 years or so only animals and perhaps a poacher or two ventured there. The land belonged to the lord of the manor and was not far from his ancient manor house, and when, in the 18th century, the gentry began to create pleasure gardens and household gardens, it seems likely that fish ponds were then built utilising the hollows of the green lane.

It must always have been a wet and damp place, and a spring rising to the south could easily be channelled into it. A long south to north pond was created with an earth dam at the northern end. On the eastern side, at a higher level is a series of ponds linked by a leat with an overflow system into the long pond. Whether the ponds were created for food or for a water garden is uncertain. But in the 1720s and 1730s it is recorded that Sir George Trenchard spent a great deal of money creating his pleasure gardens. It is a tranquil and peaceful spot, with gently sloping ground and lovely open views – just the right setting for walking and talking for the genteel 18th century ladies.

Today, the complex is lost beneath the nut trees and small silver birches and the deep pasture grasses. Wild orchids grow there and squirrels play. But its secret can still be read by the stones and banks beneath the vegetation.

One of the local village footpaths crosses fields and copses on its way to Morden. In the centre of one of these fields is a tree known locally as the Bull Oak. On it is carved a coffin, and the letters SC 1849, well visible and scored into the bark.

The story told about this is that Samuel Crumpler, who

was born in 1794, owned the field across which the footpath went, and earned the displeasure of the villagers who frequently used it, by keeping a bull there. Samuel insisted that the bull was quiet and harmless, and one day to prove his point he strolled across the field. The bull charged at him and gored him to death by the oak tree. The villagers carved the coffin and inscription as a reminder of this ironic happening. Samuel's great grandson still lives in Lytchett today, not far from that fatal Bull Oak.

Lytchett Minster

Lytchett Minster is a village one tends to drive through, and feel it is a place of little interest. It is on the A35 from Dorchester to Upton, and next time you travel this way, do not take the bypass, but venture into the village.

The church has records dating back to 1554, but the existing building was erected in 1831–33. The village has two public houses of great age, the Bakers Arms and St Peter's Finger. A depot was opened at St Peter's Finger in 1774 for the collection of Dorset buttons, which were hand made by village folk in their own homes.

This cottage industry was started in Shaftesbury in 1650 by a man called Aberham Case. Many villages had been hit by the plague, and the villagers eagerly accepted the chance of work. These buttons were made in natural coloured linen thread, which was spun from locally grown flax. The whole family could take part; children cut lengths of wire which they twisted into rings and dipped in solder. These rings were used as a base for the 'Singleton buttons', a name given to them by a local family, some of whom still reside in the parish. The children who performed this task were called dippers and winders. When the buttons were finished, the children had to sew them on to cards: pink for export, navy blue for second grade export, and yellow for those sold on the home markets.

Often food and provisions were given to the workers instead of money. One shilling and sixpence paid for a gross of buttons, rising to two shillings and sixpence for top quality buttons.

In 1781 the firm of Case Brothers bought a cottage opposite the St Peter's Finger. The new depot was a small shop attached to an old cottage considered to be about 300 years old. Attached to the other end was a stable. The whole building is now being lovingly restored by the new owners. It was built with cob walls (a mixture of mud, straw and dung), with flagstone floors laid directly on to the earth. An inglenook fire place and bread oven has been discovered in the kitchen, and the original doorway into the shop. It is thought to have had a thatched roof when first built, but this was later changed to tiles.

The button industry declined in 1851–53, due to the introduction of a machine for stamping out brass buttons. This machine was exhibited at the Great Exhibition held at the Crystal Palace. The inventor was called Ashton, and although he was not interested in making buttons himself, he was keen to sell the machine to those who were.

Unfortunately, when the industry collapsed, many people were made destitute and whole families emigrated to Canada and Australia.

In 1901 Lady Florence Lees from Lytchett Minster reopened the Old Button Shop, and the Lytchett Mission began making buttons again. The venture lasted until the First World War, when women went to work on the land and in factories to help the war effort.

Since then, the cottage and shop has had various uses. Once it was a small beer house called the Wheel; then successively a shoemaker's, pork butcher's, confectioner's, radio repairs shop and a store for books and paper.

In 1970 the present owner and a friend opened the shop once more, selling antiques. They still have a few old hand-made buttons in stock.

Marnhull

➤ Just to the right of the porch of St Gregory's church is to be found the grave of Rev Robert Bruce Kennard, rector of Marnhull 1858–1895. At its head stands a large stone cross, hung about with a heavy chain attached to an anchor, and resting at its side two large closed volumes. Author of several scholarly works, the presence of the books may be thought a not surprising decoration. The presence of an anchor would, however, seem less easy to account for since history does not reveal any nautical associations in the life of the cleric.

Apparently a person of considerable private means, the reverend gentleman financed the rebuilding of the chancel of the church, and later became the owner of Nash Court. He was also a cattle breeder of some repute, winning prizes for his herd of pedigree dairy shorthorns.

Born in 1824, Rev Kennard married his first wife in 1848 and the union was blessed with nine offspring. Three years after her death in 1878, he once again took a bride. The circumstances surrounding this event created a sensation at the time and remain shrouded in mystery. Papers of the day carried the story under the startling heading 'The Woodford Kidnapping Case' (proving that reporters' gifts for the sensational are nothing new). His chosen bride, a lady considerably younger than himself, was a Miss Marie Bade, a native of Bremen, Germany, who at the time was residing in Woodford, Essex.

On the eve of the wedding Mr Kennard travelled to Woodford to spend the night at the local Castle Hotel. Suddenly, while he was in his room awaiting dinner, a

carriage drew up outside. The driver, on entering the establishment, approached Mr Kennard with some plausible tale,
as a result of which Mr Kennard hastily left the hotel in his
company. As the brougham was about to leave two rough
characters boarded it, and it soon became apparent to Mr
Kennard that he was the victim of a kidnap plot. At the end
of the journey he was unceremoniously bundled into a
house and thrust into a downstairs room. The following
morning, after a restless night, he proceeded to bribe his
captors and thereby secured his release. On being set free he
made his way to the church, where the delayed marriage
ceremony eventually took place.

There seems to have been no action taken by the police in
regard to the alleged abduction. What can have been the
motive of his abductors? Was it indeed that those most
interested in the ultimate disposition of his estate (ie the
children of his first marriage) resolved to intervene, in the
hope that the wedding, once delayed, might never afterwards take place'. The answer, it is feared, must remain
forever 'hidden'.

St Gregory's has other stories to tell. In ancient churches in
Dorset, it is not unusual to find a tomb with the effigy of a
knight lying on top, with crossed ankles if he had taken part
in a crusade. Some have their feet resting on a dog, some
have the effigy of a wife beside them or, in Sherborne
Abbey, a son. In St Gregory's, the Carent tomb has a knight
lying comfortably between his *two* wives!

Marnhull was the village of Marriott in Thomas Hardy's
book, *Tess of the D'Urbervilles* and a thatched cottage on
which he based his description of her home is known as
Tess's Cottage, while the Crown Hotel appears in the book
as the Pure Drop Inn.

The Catholics of Marnhull have a fascinating history. In
the 16th century the new Protestant religion was not readily
accepted by everyone upon whom it was forced by the state,
and heavy fines were imposed upon those Catholics who

adhered to the old faith. Imprisonment and death was the punishment meted out to anyone giving shelter or succour to a priest attempting to minister to his stricken flock. As the years progressed the great strength of Catholicism in England was to be found among the Catholic landed gentry.

Where an estate belonged to a family faithful to the Catholic church, the servants and estate workers received some protection. These large households supported their own chaplain, and so, throughout the countryside small missions were established. Marnhull was such a mission, together with Stour Provost and Fiddleford, where Catholicism remained very vigorous.

George Hussey bought the manor of Marnhull in 1651 and came to live at Nash Court. They were a staunch Catholic family and they lived at Nash Court for more than 200 years. During that time they supported the Catholics in the village with housing, employment, a priest to minister to them, and a centre for Mass.

A second centre for Catholic worship was established in Marnhull in 1725 when Father Cornforth built a small presbytery in Old Mill Lane with a chapel up in the loft. This was maintained by a bequest from the White family of Stour Provost. Just over a hundred years later the present church of Our Lady was founded in 1832. The priest moved into the new presbytery in 1923. Traces of the gable end of the original presbytery of 1725 can still be seen in the end wall of the priory building.

The Priory of St Joseph beside the church was erected by the Canons Regular of the Lateran, an order for priests who served many of the west country parishes in what is now the Plymouth Diocese. When they built it in the 1880s it was used as a school for boys who had expressed an interest in joining the Order. After the canons left, the building was occupied between 1903 and the 1920s by three successive orders of nuns, the first two of which had come from France as refugees from the anti-religious Combes Laws. Interestingly, Marnhull had been a place of refuge a hundred years earlier, when English Benedictine nuns, fleeing the excesses of the French Revolution, had lived in Nash Court, which they leased from the Husseys between 1795 and 1807.

In 1846 the Husseys gave some land at the corner of Great Down Lane and Old Mill Lane on which a school was built. This was enlarged in 1871, and was replaced completely in 1953 by the present school next to the church. Rose Cottage in Great Down Lane is the original 1846 school building.

Melbury Abbas

In a beautiful corner of north Dorset some two miles south of Shaftesbury, lies the well known landmark, Melbury Hill. On top of that hill, over 800 ft above sea level, is Melbury Beacon. This is one of a string of fire beacons used during the reign of Elizabeth I to warn of the coming of the Spanish Armada.

As the Armada sailed up the Channel, coastal fires were lit to mark its progress. These were followed by inland fires which warned the soldiers to be ready to march. When the fleet was off Portland, Melbury Beacon was lit to warn the Wiltshire Militia – not Dorset as one would suppose – to march to Weymouth.

The beacon itself consists of three stone-lined fire holes surrounded by a circular ditch, which is Victorian in origin and was originally destined to have trees planted in it. The fire holes are well preserved and a good example of their type.

In the 20th century the beacon has been lit to celebrate Royal occasions. In 1935 it marked the Silver Jubilee of King George V and Queen Mary. Apparently, on that occasion the huge fire stack took a fortnight to build. Next came the Coronation of Queen Elizabeth II in 1953.

The Queen's Silver Jubilee in 1977 was the next event. Those unable to climb the steep side of Melbury Hill were transported by car and landrover across the downs to the beacon, where they were greeted by a huge bonfire. The Queen's health was drunk in cider. The Royal cipher and the word JUBILEE were depicted in flaming torches on the slopes of Melbury Hill. The beacon was also lit in honour of the marriage of HRH the Prince of Wales to Lady Diana Spencer in 1981 – one of a series of beacons lit throughout the country. Children's tea parties, sports and social evenings accompanied all these celebrations.

The last time the beacon was lit was on 19th July 1988 to commemorate the 400th anniversary of the Spanish Armada. At 10.17 pm a chain of beacons was lit throughout the country. About 200 people from surrounding areas attended and the huge blaze was visible for miles around. Melbury's oldest inhabitant Mr Arthur Henstridge, then aged 89, was invited to set light to the bonfire but is reported to have replied that he was not interested in remembering something which happened 400 years ago! So the honour went to another of Melbury's long-standing inhabitants, Mr Robert Blades.

Situated on National Trust land, Melbury Beacon is also in a designated area of Special Scientific Interest. It is well worth the walk entailed to reach it for the wealth of flora and fauna and for the magnificent views it affords across the Blackmore Vale.

Down a little lane, hardly more than a car's width, is Melbury Abbas mill. It is an old water-powered mill and still workable. Indeed, there has been a mill on this site since the time of the Domesday Book in 1086. Its present giant wheel, which was in daily use until 1960, is dated 1875, and the workings of it are powered by a delightful Heath Robinson affair of inter-operating wheels, angled gears, pulleys and stout, robustly crafted belts. It stands at the edge of a beautiful millpond, long since adopted by proud swans and several strains of duck, which embraces the pretty chalk stream called the river Sturkel.

There have been a tremendous number of stories told of the antics of the Home Guard during the Second World War, most at their expense. But sometimes they were the unwitting victims of practical jokes.

One winter's morning, with snow covering the ground, a woman cleaner at the rectory in Melbury Abbas thought she would have a little fun with the Home Guard to give them something to do. She reported that she had seen paratroopers coming down onto the hill. Immediately the system swung into action. The Commander in Chief ordered all of the Home Guard to assemble at the bottom of Zig Zag Hill. One man, who had been gritting Spreadeagle Hill, asked someone to look after his horse and return him to the mill if he wasn't home by teatime. Then he went home, picked up his Browning automatic and about 500 rounds of ammunition and, not forgetting his lunch box, assembled with the rest.

Major Sampson ordered Dick Mullins to take two men up Zig Zag Hill to see what they could find. The rest of the Home Guard were spread out along the bottom of the hill to East Melbury Farm, with orders to fire if they saw movement. One young man, seeing figures moving on the hill, wanted to open fire, but, luckily for Dick Mullins and his men, a more experienced sergeant recognised his friends. The hill was thoroughly searched but, of course, nothing was found.

But the story did not end there, for soon hundreds of regular soldiers could be seen coming through the valley from Spreadeagle, searching as they came. Meanwhile in the village, the Artillery had assembled, sent out from Yeovil. By this time it was dark and, as nothing had been found, everyone went home. The same evening, Lord Haw Haw, in his daily propaganda broadcast from Germany, reported the landing of paratroopers on the Shaftesbury Downs! Years later the lady at the bottom of all this told one of the members of the Home Guard what she had done. Little did she realise the havoc she would cause when she decided to have a little fun with the Melbury Abbas Home Guard.

Melbury Bubb

Melbury Bubb is a remote, attractive little village, not far from the Somerset border.

In the lovely little church of St Mary, nestling in the hillside, there is a curious and strangely beautiful stone font.

'Upside down' Saxon font at Melbury Bubb

It is wonderfully carved, depicting stags and serpents – but they are all upside down! It is believed that the font was once part of an ancient round shaft or sculptured cross, hollowed out by the Normans for use within the church. Was the 'upside down' motif a deliberate decision, or was it a mistake by the Norman mason? It would be fascinating to know.

The church has other interesting features, particularly its stained glass. One window commemorates Walter Bokeler, the 15th century rector who saw the church tower built.

Melbury Osmond

Imagine the fingers holding a needle threaded with brightly coloured wool, and the hand rising and falling in rhythm as the needle clips the canvas and a stitch is made. It takes around 25,000 stitches and 100 hours to complete one church kneeler. Since 1975 nearly 100 hassocks have been lovingly completed for St Osmond's church here in Melbury Osmond.

They make an interesting study, depicting different scenes and themes of village life. Not all have been created in the little thatched cottages and farms of the vicinity. One was worked near the deserts of Saudi Arabia, in an air-conditioned house in distant Jeddah. This shows the altar, flowers and initials, in memory of a baby son, buried in the churchyard. Another kneeler was created in a busy little Suffolk town, near the Norfolk Broads. This one depicts a helicopter flying over Melbury. The embroiderer's husband was a helicopter engineer and her son is a pilot.

A farm scene is shown on one hassock, with the farmer and his wife, now both at rest in 'God's Acre' outside. An animal lover has chosen hedgehogs, which are often seen in the village gardens. Twenty or more very beautiful hassocks were worked by one lady who loved needlework and devoted many hours of her later years, between the ages of 70 and 80, to this noble task.

The most intricate hassock of all shows the Ilchester coat of arms, designed by the embroiderer in tent stitch, and won first prize at a WI county festival.

Much could be written, as each kneeler tells a story – a dove of peace for a daughter's wedding in 1977, a bold Union Jack for the Jubilee, and bells for the bellringers. A list of subjects, with the embroiderer's name, can be found at the entrance to the church. Come and kneel awhile.

Lovers of Hardy will also find interest in the knowledge that his mother was baptised and married in this little church, and is thought to have been born in the little Barton Cottage to the north of the west door.

Milton on Stour

Pernes, or Purns Mill as it is now called, is on the Shreen, which flows a mile distant from the centre of Milton proper, in the district called Colesbrooke.

Originally named Redding Mill, it came into the Pernes family of Bowridge some time in the 16th century, when it was probably re-christened. It was then a grist mill for grinding corn for local farmers, relying on power from the fast-flowing Shreen river, which rises in the chalk downs above Mere.

The land and mill were bequeathed to Richard Perne by his mother about the beginning of the 17th century. Also in her will Rachel Perne left to her maidservant, Alice Clement, '. . . one cow, my best gown, the best of my petticoats and the jacket I wore when executing this will'. It is intriguing to learn that seven months after his mother died in 1651, Richard, a bachelor who had lived with his mother through her 20 years of widowhood, married her servant Alice at St Mary's church, Gillingham.

With Richard Perne's death, the mill appears to have been sold, but the surrounding land – the Linchees fields, were retained by the family. The ownership from then on is somewhat vague, although we know that in 1770 a certain William Tinney, who married Miss Mary Perne, was in charge of the mill. There was a serious fire in 1825 at the mill, but before this Matthew Parham had bought it from the Tinney family, and it was he who rebuilt Purns Mill.

After inheriting the mill, his daughter Charlotte put it up for auction in 1850. The *Western Gazette* advertisement described it thus –

'Purns Mill, Gillingham, with residence, a flour mill with three pairs of stones, a jute and tow-spinning factory, two stories in height, capable of working 800 heavy spindles, with cording room and engine and boiler house adjoining'.

The head of another distinguished local family, George Blandford Matthews, whose forebears had been brewing in Wyke since 1773, bought it, then married Charlotte Parham and moved into the Old House at Milton. G. B. Matthews converted the mill into a maltings for his brewery and a grain store, since he continued flour-milling. It was hoped to attract business from South Wiltshire and North Dorset farmers by processing their wheat and barley, but the venture did not flourish and Matthews and his partner, Henry Kaines, a solicitor, saw their capital depreciate seriously, mainly due to competition from local roller mills and imports of American flour.

In 1933 the limited liability company which operates the mill today, was formed. Such is the mill's history, but its claim to international fame is that it was sketched and painted several times by John Constable, RA.

John Constable had an especial fondness for river scenes and watermills; so it was not surprising that when his close friend, Archdeacon Fisher, came from Berkshire to become vicar of Gillingham in 1819, he should get Constable to visit him here and also ensure that the artist was shown the local mills. Happily it was Purns Mill which impressed him the most. The first visit took place in 1820, but probably Constable did not even sketch the mill at that time; nevertheless subsequent correspondence between vicar and painter disclosed Constable's interest in it. In 1823 he wrote to the vicar, saying, 'I want to do something at that famous mill, a mile or two off'. The same year he came to Milton and must have made several visits to the mill site.

From the work that Constable must have completed in the open air around Purns Mill, only a small sketch in oils is known to survive in a private collection. It depicts the mill from a south-west aspect, and undoubtedly formed the basis for two paintings of Purns Mill, or Parham's Mill, which Constable later completed in his studio. In 1824 one version of Parham's Mill was completed for Archdeacon Fisher, and it has survived to be on display at the Fitzwilliam Museum in Cambridge. A second version was painted in 1826 for a certain Mrs Hands, when he was holidaying in Brighton; this painting has found its way to the Yale Center for British Art in the USA.

It is assumed that Constable made other open air studies of the mill in 1823, and one of these untraced sketches would have been used to paint a third study of Purns Mill from the west; it was completed in 1827. It remained unsold on John Constable's death, and eventually was acquired by the Victoria and Albert Museum in London. It is thought that this version was commissioned by the Tinney family, who owned the mill between about 1770 and 1820. John Tinney being a friend of the Archdeacon had been introduced to Constable by John Fisher, but he never received the painting. The artist held his 1826 and 1827 versions of *Parham Mill* in high esteem and exhibited them at the Royal Academy in the years of their completion. In 1826 after finishing his first version, he wrote to Fisher from Brighton, saying, 'I did there one of my best pictures – the subject was the mill (Perne's) at Gillingham – it is about two feet and is so very rich and pleasing.'

The timing of Constable's visits to Purns Mill were particularly fortunate for, in the late summer of 1825 the disastrous fire occurred there. The Archdeacon wrote angrily to Constable –

'Matthew Parham's (alias Perne's) Mill is burned to the ground, and exists only on your canvas. A huge, misshapen, new, bright, brick, modern, improved, patent monster is starting up in its stead'.

Constable reacts predictably –

'I am vexed at the fate of the poor old mill. There will soon be an end to the picturesque in the kingdom'.

How very fortunate that one of the greatest landscape artists of all time should have preserved the original mill on canvas for our enjoyment.

Moreton

There is a treasure here in Moreton. It is believed that the church of St Nicholas must be the only one in the world to possess windows entirely of engraved glass. The theme of 'light' has been followed to produce a setting of great beauty and artistry.

The church itself was rebuilt by James Frampton in 1776 and then was remodelled and enlarged during the 19th century. Several of the windows were at that time of stained glass, created by Thomas Williment, one of the best stained glass artists of the time.

St Nicholas' church, Moreton

It was on the evening of 8th October 1940 that tragedy struck. A bomb fell close to the north wall, destroying the wall and blasting out the window glass and interior decoration. Many villagers must have wondered, on seeing the devastation in the cold light of day, whether their much loved church would ever recover.

For several years the villagers worshipped in the hall at Moreton House, while work went on to rebuild and restore St Nicholas's. When you stand in the churchyard now, such was the skill of the builders, it is well nigh impossible to discern where the old and new meet. In May 1950 the church was rededicated.

The windows are the creation of Laurence Whistler, and have been installed as a result of private commissions at intervals since the 1950s. The first were the five in the apse. Candles wound with ribbon carry Bible quotations, while

99

medallions depict the church, harvest on land and at sea, the emblems of the Passion, a Christmas tree and an ash tree. Twenty years passed before the next window was installed, but since then the designs have become even more lyrical and flowing, while still keeping to the theme of 'light'.

Burials in the churchyard ceased in 1930 and a new cemetery was opened on the west side of the Moreton to Wool road. Here lies buried T. E. Lawrence, 'Lawrence of Arabia'. He was killed in a motor cycle accident near Clouds Hill in 1935.

Motcombe

The boundaries of Motcombe parish push right up the steep hillside to the very edge of Shaftesbury. On that hillside stand the fields of Cowherd Shute Farm. Left as grazing pasture and hay meadows, and farmed in the traditional way, they retain a wealth of wild flowers.

One meadow with the evocative name of Summer Ground has a patch of bluebells in one area where the slope is too steep for the hay cutter. Villagers await hay making time with special interest. Years ago, when gipsies were in the habit of calling at farms seeking employment, they were on one particular occasion refused work by the then farmer at Cowherd Shute Farm. The gipsies responded, it is said, by putting a curse on Summer Ground. When the hay is cut they warned, it would rain. And it invariably does!

Those newly engaged on repair work on their properties in the village are often intrigued to find old building bricks stamped with a letter. From one point of view it could be an 'M'. Since in earlier times there were many small local brickworks, and knowing of the existence of such a site on the outskirts of the village, it is sometimes thought that it is 'M' for Motcombe. However, reverse the brick and it reads as a 'W'. This gives the clue to the history of the village, since with neighbouring Shaftesbury it formed part of the Westminster estate. The present Duke of Westminster is England's wealthiest landowner, including in his estate large tracts of Central London.

The Marquis of Westminster resided at old Motcombe House, later destroyed by fire and rebuilt early in the 20th century. The house may have been built in Motcombe rather than in the larger Shaftesbury because of the lack of water in that hilltop town. Residents of Shaftesbury had to seek rights to water from parishes under the hill, particularly from Enmore Green. Certainly Motcombe Park occupies a much more sheltered site than the exposed hill top.

Much of the parish showed the influence of the Westminsters. All the old field gates had a 'W' carved into the woodwork. Sadly none of these remain. Curiously, the Marquis could not claim the road through Motcombe Park as a private road because a corpse had once been carried along it for burial at nearby Enmore Green.

During the Marquis' time the village was much changed. The village school was built in 1839 and the church rebuilt in 1846. The Marchioness gave annual gifts to the estate families; locally made boots for the men, and red flannel for the women to make into petticoats.

The last Marchioness of Westminster lies buried in an ironrailed tomb in the village churchyard. Nearby are the graves of descendants, the Grosvenors and the Stalbridges – the latter being the last to use Motcombe House as a family home. One family member, Lady Theodora Guests, laid down rules for the local schoolgirls. They were allowed no ribbons in their hair, no curls showing from under their bonnets and no lace on their dresses!

All of this is now history but small reminders remain. In south west London you can find Motcomb Street near Grosvenor Place. And down in Motcombe there are still the bricks . . .

Nether and Over Compton

➤ In recent years village children, at dusk, would climb the hill to Tucker's Cross (as it is still known) and, standing in the lane and clutching each other for safety, would chant 'Tucker, Tucker, come out Tucker' and then run for their lives down to the village before it got dark – they were not really sure who Tucker was or why he was there!

An extract from parish records makes all clear however. 'Robert Tucker, a notorious bad character, hung himself in his bakehouse chamber early on the morning of Sunday, the 30th April, aged nearly 71. Buried on Tuesday the 2nd May at midnight in the Crop Road on the righthand side of Ginnygore Gate, a field of arable land belonging to the Rector of Nether Compton, 1820'.

In Nether Compton, situated at Cromwell Hill (so called because Cromwell is supposed to have had his horses shod at the old forge there), is a high stone wall with a handsome doorway. This is the entrance to a graveyard – now closed – belonging to the nonconformist chapel built on the outskirts of the village.

The doorway was built with a bequest from John Hopkins Esq, of London, who died in 1732 and who was nicknamed 'Vulture' Hopkins. He left £100 to 'repair the wall of and make a gateway to the burial place of the Dissenters near Sherborne, Dorsetshire'.

There is a fine table top tomb in this now sadly overgrown graveyard.

The battle of Babylon Hill was fought on 7th September 1642 between the Royalists from Sherborne and the Parliamentarians from Yeovil. The combatants of this indecisive battle must have passed through the parishes of Over and Nether Compton, but there is no mention of casualties in the parish records. The battle field lies partly in Over Compton and partly in Bradford Abbas.

In 1645, when General Fairfax led his victorious Parliamentarian army through the South West in a mopping up exercise, he is believed to have stabled his horses in Nether Compton church, and, at Cromwell's orders, burned any 'idolatrous furnishings' of the church. There is a mark on the outside wall (between the base of the tower and the porch) where a fire was lit and it is believed in the village that this was the spot where the burning took place.

An extract from the *Dorset County Chronicle* on 2nd October 1913 reads: 'Gruesome Discovery. During recent quarrying operations at a quarry situated on the left side of Halfway House Hill on the road from Sherborne to Yeovil, workmen discovered the skeleton of a human being. The gruesome relic when first discovered, was found to be intact except that the shin bone of one leg was broken in two places. One of the District Council's workmen first saw what he afterwards discovered to be the bones of a foot, and in view of the fact that four or five other skeletons have been unearthed during recent years in the same quarry, exercised great care in removing the soil and limestone and eventually found the skeleton which had been placed face upwards on a bed of rock, some two and a half feet below the surface.'

The paper goes on to suggest that this was a soldier who perhaps fell in battle or who was in the Siege of Sherborne Castle. It seems most likely that he was killed at Babylon Hill, which is near at hand.

On Oak Apple Day (29th May), in memory of the Restoration of the Monarchy, the Nether Compton bell ringers ring the church bells in the village of Trent, the neighbouring village. Why is unclear. King Charles, as we all know, hid at Trent Manor for many days but it seems that the Trent villagers were not royalists. However, neither were the Compton inhabitants! Perhaps the Trent ringers had celebrated too much at the time – anyway the tradition still holds and the ringers of Compton still make their annual pilgrimage.

Robert Goodden of Compton House, Over Compton extended and restored Over Compton church at his own expense in 1822. It is a delightful building with a triple decker pulpit and hatchments of the Goodden family. There are also several stones let into the walls in remembrance of estate employees – perhaps a little unusual.

The finest feature of the church is a life sized statue of Robert Goodden. He stands in the family pew wearing country clothes and until very recently leaning on a stick (it is hoped to repair this soon). The inscription, written by himself, reads 'Robert Goodden born in this Parish 24th August 1751, beautified this church 1822. This statue erected 1825 died 3rd October 1828'. The statue, having been erected, was boarded up for three years until he died. How strange to sit in the family pew every Sunday knowing what was standing beside you, waiting for your death! Tradition is that on every festival the statue is given a button hole of whatever flower is in season. The village children used to be quite sure that this life-like statue climbed down off its plinth at night and walked around the village!

Okeford Fitzpaine

Okeford Fitzpaine is set in one of the loveliest areas of Dorset, described by Thomas Hardy as 'The Vale of the Little Dairies'. It is the country of *Tess of the D'Urbervilles.*

The short turf was full of moss, and moss gathering was once a thriving industry in the village. It was to be found growing on Okeford and Belchalwell Hill, and sometimes further afield on Fontmell Downs. From here, there are extensive views of neat villages and the Blackmore Vale. 'Mossing' was popular with the children, who joined in as helpers. Given a chance, there was time for fun and games on the hillside. The buyers were Covent Garden merchants, who sent letters or telegrams when they wanted supplies. This was the signal for the mossers to gather on the hill with their rakes, which were small garden rakes, with turned down prongs. But some villagers used their bare hands to gather the moss, working down hill.

Having raked the moss, it was then tied into small bundles with 'tiers', which were made by cutting a sack along the seams, and unpicking the threads. This was often a task for the children. One hundred and forty four bundles were then packed into sack-bags, with twelve layers of twelve bundles tied at the top. These were laid under a gorse bush, or similar shade, until ready for collection. They were then labelled and loaded on wagons, and taken to Shillingstone railway station for consignment to London.

The boys would have a fine time sliding the sacks down the hill, using them as sledges. Good sport to see who could be the fastest. Sometimes the mossers had bad weather with snow covering the ground, but that did not deter them. The snow was cleared away with boards tied to their rakes, and the moss gathered as usual. There was one good friend to the mossers, and that was the rabbit, who kept the moss patches free from grass, brambles and weeds. Myxamatosis almost wiped them out in the 1950s.

With the changing pattern of agriculture, mossing declined. Today Okeford Hill is partly enclosed with cattle and sheep grazing, and motor-bike scrambles are frequently held where children played and moss was gathered. But the air is still sweet, and the views are still beautiful.

Okeford Fitzpaine seems to have been particularly rich in nicknames. There was 'Tacker' Young, the shoe repairer, and 'Old Shepherd' was well known. Even his wife was better known as 'Mrs Shepherd', than by her married name.

There was 'Whyderwhy' who was always asking questions; 'Duck Legs' who walked with a waddle; and Jimmy Head was known as 'Jimmy Nut'. Ole Brush 'Andle' worked in the general store. George 'Bellows' had the habit of puffing out his cheeks as a conversation opening. And Mr Rose was 'Champy Rose' – everything in his conversation was 'real champion'!

Poole – Lilliput

This oddly named district in Poole owes its name to a rogue of the 18th century – Isaac Gulliver. Swift's satiric book *Gulliver's Travels* had been published in 1726, and the imaginary kingdom of Lilliput had soon taken a hold on the public imagination.

Smuggling was a way of life in the 18th century. Poole was notorious for crime of every degree and smuggling appeared easy. The sandy lane leading from Poole to Sandbanks was bordered by reeds, wild grasses and salt marshes and of course much heathland; all ideal to hide contraband and in the dark of a winter's night, small boats were able to land. If anyone living in the few cottages along this path heard anything in the night, they would obviously put their heads under the covers, as they often benefited from the action of the smugglers.

Gulliver first came to the attention of the Revenue authorities when he was twelve years old; he was then a smuggler's assistant. By the time he was 18, he was supplying markets over a wide area and depriving the Revenue of many thousands of pounds.

He was born on 5th September 1745 at a place called Semington and he married Elizabeth Beale of Thorney Down in 1768. They married in the church of St Mary the Virgin at Sixpenny Handley. His father-in-law kept the inn at Thorney Down and seems to have become fond of Isaac Gulliver. Soon after moving in, it was advertised that post chaises could be hired there to go to London and elsewhere. This, it would appear, was to cover the many horses needed by

Gulliver. Over the years Mr and Mrs Gulliver had three children – two girls and a boy (named Isaac).

In 1778 Gulliver was in trouble regarding nine casks of brandy and 16 hundred weight of tea which had disappeared. It is said that he was conveyed in a barrel through Poole to avoid capture. After this he moved his family to Longham where he set himself up as a wine and spirit merchant and sold his horses. He stayed there for several years. Kinson at this time became notorious for smuggling and the locals, it was said, were 'smugglers to a man'. This appeared to suit Gulliver, who continued to keep out of the hands of the Revenue officers and by the 1780s was in control of smuggling from Lymington to Torbay and to the Channel Islands. Goods from France were tax free on the Islands.

On 3rd May 1782, the King declared a free pardon to all seamen 'Be they smugglers or outlaws in jail or overseas' on condition they joined the Navy or provided seamen to serve in the Navy.

Isaac Gulliver seems to have taken advantage of this and quite soon was living in a house called Flag Farm at Lilliput, looking over lovely Evening Hill. He had become a very, very rich man when he moved to Wimborne. His two daughters married well, but his son died aged 23 years. Gulliver died, ironically, on Friday 13th September 1822, aged 77 years. He was buried in Wimborne Minster and his memorial stone is in the centre aisle. He left his wife and children very well provided for indeed. He appears to have been a remarkable man and it is said 'he was a prince amongst smugglers', reviled only by the Revenue officers.

Portland

➤ The continuity of Portland's Court Leet has remained unbroken since long before Norman times. Its powers and functions, titles and administrations are unimpaired to the present day, much to the chagrin of the local Council.

True, the officers and members of the Court no longer meet at the Jacobean George Inn in Reforne, nor do they smoke their long churchwarden pipes. But the procedure is the same as centuries ago and grievances are heard and ancient laws and tenants' rights upheld.

Portland's Court Leet is a Crown Court, with no intermediaries between the reigning monarch and the tenants. Whatever differences concerning the Crown or Commons' land may arise, are still dealt with and settled directly to the satisfaction of both parties, remembering that under ancient laws only the soil is the Crown's. The herbage is the tenant's, to graze cattle or harvest as he will.

It is the function of the Court Leet to safeguard all Common lands on the island, all verges and seemingly waste lands. Nothing may be erected, neither houses or huts, telegraph poles or electricity standards without the Court's permission and due compensation given.

Walls and fences around the Common lands must be kept in good order and such fines as may be imposed are distributed by the Court Leet to island charities, along with the monies accruing from His Majesty's (King Charles II) grant of a small levy on every ton of stone taken from the quarries.

The Court Leet is elected only from the tenants, a certain number of whom are summoned each November to form the 'Jury and the Homage' and are under penalty to attend. This is done by the Crown Steward or his deputy representing Her Majesty and he swears in the Jury in ancient form. A foreman is appointed and all persons who since last court have 'digged or taken stone from the demesne must render under oath an account thereof . . .'

This concerns both Crown and tenants but all other business involves only the tenants so the Steward retires and the Foreman takes the chair.

The officers of the Court are then appointed. They include the Reeve, the Chief Constable, his deputies called Inspectors, and the Haywards, whose duty it is to see that no cattle from the fields stray on to the Common land and so safeguard its grazing rights.

Then the Affeerors are appointed to assess the penalties of fines of those whose improper working of quarries, deposit of rubble, encroachment or failure to maintain their fence or walls has brought their cases to light.

Then comes the more pleasurable task of allocating funds to local charities. Business being finished, the Crown Steward is recalled, the court findings are read out to him and the report signed by each member of the Jury. The Steward then closes the Court until the next year.

There are many cases of Court Leets being held in England, but the proceedings are mainly ornamental, the officers having neither powers nor functional duties. Portland's active Court Leet has been threatened once or twice but faithful and loyal Portlanders, realising that without some such tribunal Common Rights might be lost, have saved and preserved its function for all time, alongside its redundant old church of St George with its twin pulpit and enclosed pew seats.

Ryme Intrinseca

The founder of the Quakers, George Fox, toured the country in 1668 to set up 'Meetings in Discipline'. Arriving in Dorset, he stopped at Ryme Intrinseca and lodged with Michael Blanchard, a Huguenot. There he held the first Quaker meeting in Dorset. Forty nine friends came from all over the county, representing 17 communities.

The remains of a Quaker burial ground can still be seen in a field at Ryme. It is said that six bodies are buried there, but only one crooked gravestone remains. The inscription is almost illegible, just the word 'Here . .' and a carved cherub's head.

Seatown

Seatown was once a thriving fishing village and harbourage, which is probably why the local inn is called the 'Anchor'. In previous centuries the approach from the shore was not precipitous, but gradual, which explains why, when smuggling was at its height, it was necessary to have local coastguards. Watch House, on the cliff top, was where the families of the guards lived, and the Guard House was the coast guard station; both of these are now private dwellings. The Watch House is now right on the edge of the cliff, whereas at one time it had a big lawn and garden in front.

The fish house, where the men used to store their gear and the odd boat in the winter, stood where the toilets are now. Older residents can recall the lovely smell of tar! If it rained when one was at Seatown, the men were very choosy about who they allowed to shelter inside!

In the 19th century more than 40 fishermen were operating from Seatown, also adding to their income by smuggling. Many tales are told of the brandy that was run in, the different hills and clumps of trees being the markers, to drop the contraband offshore until safe for a landing.

At Chideock and Seatown practically every family was involved in the trade. Some women conveyed the French liquor from the shore to the hide-out in small casks hidden beneath their crinolines, and one preventive officer remarked that it was surprising how often the local women became pregnant. Roadstead Farm had a secret room used for storing the spirits, and another room was found beneath a false floor at the old Mill House.

The morning of Thursday, 11th June 1685, was the start of the Monmouth rebellion. Three men were rowed ashore from the 200 ton ship *Helderenburgh*, while the main body of men landed at Lyme Regis. The men who landed at Seatown distributed 'neats tongues and bottles of canary' to the long-shore men who beached them. Neats tongues were ox-tongues. A customs man living in Chideock heard of the landings, and sent a message post haste to King James in London. He was suitably rewarded. This robbed the rebels of the element of surprise. It is possible, had the initial landings at Seatown not taken place, the 'Bloody Assizes' presided over by Judge Jefferies might never have been held.

During the First World War, on 1st January 1915, *HMS Formidable* was sunk in the bay. Many bodies were washed ashore along the coast. Two came ashore at Seatown, and are buried in St Giles' churchyard. The War Graves Commission still visit them.

In the late 1800s a regatta was held here every summer. Up until the 1970s there were boats and men with seine nets, waiting and watching on the cliff top for the mackerel to come. Unfortunately now, owing to the shortage of fish, only shore anglers can be found on the beach.

Pebble picking has been allowed since the Second World War. To start with they were picked by hand, but now a tractor collects them, and they are taken away for grading, then used as grinding stones in the manufacture of pottery, make-up and toothpaste! The local people believe that this had added to the erosion of the shoreline, and extraction is no longer permitted by the County Council.

To the west is Golden Cap, and the rocks beneath, at low tide, can make a nice walk to St Gabriel's and Charmouth. The 'Fairy Pool' was man made. A French mud barge went ashore there in the 1920s and had to be blown up, making the pool for prawn fishing and paddling.

Shaftesbury

Since time began, high on its windy hill, Shaftesbury has gazed serenely across to Glastonbury Tor. A thousand years ago, King Alfred chose the site to build a magnificent abbey. It became one of the wealthiest houses in England, and it was said that if the Abbot of Glaston were to wed the Abbess of Shaston, their heirs would own more land than the King of England.

To the abbey in AD 978, they brought the body of the young Kind Edward after he had been murdered by his stepmother at Corfe Castle. A modern shrine has been erected to his memory in the abbey ruins. King Canute died here in 1035 and here the wife of Robert Bruce was held hostage during the wars with the Scots. The young Katherine of Aragon was a guest at the abbey on her journey from Plymouth to marry her first husband, Prince Arthur, and it was her second husband, King Henry VIII, who ordered the surrender of the abbey in 1539.

For the next 300 years, the people of Shaftesbury built their homes with abbey stones, the huddled cottages bearing silent witness to past grandeur. The remnants of the great foundation stand in a peaceful walled garden on Park Walk.

St Peter's church is the oldest church in Shaftesbury, the tower probably dates from the 13th century and contains a vaulted Tudor porch. For many years the crypt was used as a beer cellar to the old Sun and Moon Inn which, with its distinctive sign, has now become a private house attached to the Town Museum. Situated at the top of Gold Hill, the Town Museum contains among other things the gaily decorated Byzant which was presented to the lord of the manor of Gillingham together with a raw calf's head, a penny loaf, a gallon of ale and a pair of gloves, for the right to draw water from the wells in Enmore Green.

The great rampart wall of the abbey forms the boundary of Gold Hill with its cobbles and the straggle of picturesque cottages which lead down to the village of St James, which was home to those on whom the abbey depended for its services. The Abbey Farm known as Holyrood lies across the fields close to the site of the old fish ponds, and along to the west a charming group of cottages clusters around the old well head on the green of St Andrew's Pump Yard. Further along are the lanes named for the services they provided, the tanyard and the laundry.

In the 17th century, the Quaker Society of Friends built a meeting house in St James, and in a private garden is the Friends' burial ground, where Harriet and William and others have rested peacefully for 300 years.

The climb up the old Saxon walk known as Stoney Path leads back to the town with its glorious views over Cranborne Chase.

To readers of Thomas Hardy, the town will be remembered as the Shaston of *Jude the Obscure* where Old Grove's Place, now Ox House, and the school, now converted to attractive homes, are still to be found.

St Andrew's Pump Yard, Shaftesbury

Sherborne

The Castleton Water Wheel once formed an important part of Sherborne's water supply system. Using water from the nearby Oborne streams and from the lake at Sherborne Castle, its task was to drive a set of pumps which in turn pumped fresh water from a borehole adjacent to the pump-house, to the reservoir on the north side of the town. This water wheel and its predecessor carried out this function from 1869 to approximately 1960. Following a period of disuse, the pumps were scrapped but the huge water wheel, having less value to the scrap merchant, fortunately survived.

The wheel, 26 ft in diameter by 3 ft 9 ins broad, was fed with water from three different levels and from three separate sources, driving a set of three-throw ram pumps. It was capable of delivering 7,200 gallons of water per hour to the reservoir.

In the early 1970s there were proposals to save the water wheel by local councillors, but little was done. The owners, Wessex Water Authority, offered the Castleton site to the West Mill Restoration Society, which already leased the remains of a corn mill on the other side of town, but it was unable to accept. However, the then chairman of the West Mill group managed to interest three local people in the site and the Castleton Water Wheel Restoration Society was formed.

This group have been working to restore the wheel, and the site was opened to the public in 1985. Work is still going on and when sufficient components have been obtained, the wheel will be working again.

The West Mill is the last surviving water mill of the 15 which used to stand on the stretch of the river Yeo near Sherborne. A mill is marked on old maps on the site at the end of West Mill Lane as early as 1574, when the area was part of the estates of the Bishop of Salisbury. Above medieval foundations the present equipment dates from the 19th century, the last miller retiring in 1957.

Twenty years of neglect were ended in 1976 when some boys came across the mill and the Restoration Society was founded. Since then a great deal of work has been done. The external structure and first floor have been rebuilt and the bread ovens and wheel restored.

In 1979 the mill was listed as a building of historical and architectural importance by the Department of the Environment. The Society hopes eventually to be able to establish a mill museum there.

Those who love medieval buildings are spoilt for choice in this beautiful town. The abbey, castles and school are well documented, but perhaps less famous is the almshouse of St John the Baptist and St John the Evangelist. The present almshouse is older than any other building in Sherborne, except the abbey and the castles.

Other earlier charitable institutions for the care of the aged poor and infirm preceded it. The earliest was built by Brother John, the almoner of the monastery, in or about the year 1223 as a house of mercy, the name given to an almshouse in medieval times. It was originally a hospital of the order of St Augustine. The almshouse was to take two poor men and four poor women from amongst elderly local citizens, to be cared for by a housewife, to feed and wash for them. They chose a prior between themselves to obtain order and thus they lived 'till death and judgement'. They wore a uniform until some 20 years ago. On election they were required to bequeath their moveable goods for the use of the house. A later house was founded in 1448 by Robert Neville, Bishop of Sarum and was dedicated to St John the Baptist and St John the Evangelist. It is now called St John's House.

The inmates attended mass each day when the bell was rung, which it still is to this day. They also attended the public abbey church, walking in twos. If any of them were found guilty of cursing or swearing, of drunkenness or

115

St John's almshouse, Sherborne

promoting strife and debate, the offender was expelled. This code of rules and order is set up in the entrance hall.

In medieval times every mid-summer night, the custom was to hang a garland on the door in memory of John the Baptist. This custom has been restored and a garland of fresh flowers is hung in the courtyard on the 24th June each year.

St John's house is open to the public on certain days in the year and the uniform previously worn can be seen at the local museum.

A happy event took place in June 1905, when the town celebrated the twelve hundredth anniversary of its Bishopric by staging a great pageant in the Old Castle grounds. It was an ambitious undertaking for a small town of 6,000 people, and one which to judge by the press coverage stirred the national imagination and set the fashion for large scale pageants elsewhere.

What was particularly remarkable was the enthusiasm with which the whole population gave freely of their time

116

and talents. Eight hundred performers had to be clothed in period costumes and the local silk mills produced rolls of silk and satin for the richer garments, and parties of ladies were formed to make them up. A stand of seats for 2,500 people was erected and there was also standing room for many more. Altogether over 25,000 people saw the four performances.

Eleven episodes from the town's history were depicted, from the coming of St Aldhelm to that of Sir Walter Raleigh, interspersed with songs and dances accompanied by a large orchestra. Most of the songs and music were written by local people.

To show thanks to the townfolk who worked hard for the occasion, the council gave a piece of land near the railway station to create a garden for all to enjoy. It was called the Pageant Gardens, and is still much used by anyone and everyone to meet friends and have a chat. In past years a band played in the bandstand on Sundays for entertainment but sadly it is only used now for special and memorial occasions.

Shillingstone

They used to hold May Day on 9th June here, which was a great day of festival in Shillingstone for several centuries. The maypole, said at one time to be the tallest in England, was garlanded with flowers, and around the maypole dancing was kept up till far into the night. Besides the dancing there were booths, coconut shies, cheap jacks and all the fun of the fair. Even after the custom of dancing round the maypole died out, wreaths of flowers were still hung upon it and allowed to remain until they withered.

Another very old custom was the Christmas Bull. The Bull, with shaggy head and horns complete, shaggy coat and eyes of glass, was wont to appear uninvited at any Christmas celebration. None knew when he might or might not appear. He was given the freedom of every house, and allowed to penetrate into any room escorted by his keeper. The whole company would flee before his formidable horns, the more so as, towards the end of the evening, neither the Bull nor his keeper could be certified as strictly sober. The Christmas Bull was active up to the beginning of the 20th century.

The Somerset and Dorset Railway was opened in 1863. Slow and doubtful, the villagers called it, but it was held in high regard all the same. A tea party was held at the rectory barn on the day of the opening and a general holiday was enjoyed by all.

For many villagers it opened up a whole new world. The two milk factories at Shillingstone and Okeford Fitzpaine transported their milk and butter to the station by horse and cart. Hay and cattle were sent from the farms, and moss pickers used it to transport their bags of moss. And with luxury waiting rooms and a real coal fire to sit round, what did it matter if the train was late! Sadly the railway is closed now, but the station is still there, a reminder of times past.

Sixpenny Handley

How did it get its name? There was a story at one time that the village had been sold for sixpence. Not so. Actually it comes from the old Saxon – saxpenna meaning hilltop and hanlega meaning at the high clearing.

Unfortunately Sixpenny Handley has the reputation of being one of the ugliest villages in Dorset. There was a fire on 20th May 1892, when about one third of the village was destroyed in five hours. Due to a difference of opinion, the fund which had been raised to help rebuilding, went to the Chancery instead. The rebuilding that did take place was very haphazard, with corrugated iron huts going up. Most of them have disappeared now, but Sixpenny Handley still cannot be called a pretty village.

The church, however, is well worth coming to see. It has stood at the top of the village for about 900 years and is built of flint and stone. It was enlarged in 1876–78, but the tower, chancel and porch are still the original parts of the church.

Two of the windows have carved corbels on the outside. One shows a man in a ruff and a hooded lady with a wide collar. The other has a rather fierce looking fox and a sleepy looking hound.

The four original gargoyles on the tower are thought to represent the four evangelists – a man for St Matthew, a lion for St Mark, an ox for St Luke, and for St John an eagle. They are believed to have been made in Normandy in the 12th or 13th century and imported to this country.

In the south aisle is a large canopied tomb of the Alie family. The tomb has two Tuscan columns, which are characteristic of early Elizabethan monuments. There are two shields, which bore the arms of the Alies impaling the Constantine arms, but these have been rubbed smooth as if by a mason.

On the base of the tomb is a circular heraldic device, also bearing the Alie coat of arms. This stone was missing for many years. A stonemason in Wareham found it in his workshop and it was returned to Sixpenny Handley only by a chance conversation with a villager. It had been gone for over 40 years. It is thought that it was probably sent for cleaning, and was then forgotten.

In the parish register is a record of the marriage of Isaac Gulliver to the daughter of the innkeeper at Thorney Down. Gulliver, a notorious smuggler, used Handley churchyard to hide his spoils.

Against the rear wall of the churchyard near the gate, there is a tombstone with an inscription which tells how, when deer poaching was common, the carcases were hidden in an empty tomb.

Southbourne

Southbourne's Shell House is situated on the overcliff drive with a clear view of the sea. The display is the work of the late George Howard and was started in 1948. He was a friendly man who could often be seen sitting outside his house chatting to the public who had come to admire his work.

There are many items of interest. One is a boat made out of coal, reminding him of his early working days down the coal mines in Poland. He was a man with a sense of humour, as you can see as you walk around. He also had a love for little children. See if you can spot the child's necklace. The story was that a little girl walking round the Shell House fell and broke her beads. Gathering them, she asked Mr Howard if he could find a home for them. He kindly did so and made a little girl very happy.

Mr and Mrs Howard sailed the world and he was at one time a sea captain travelling on Russian convoys. This no doubt started his interest in shell collecting. The shells vary in size, some small and some big enough to sit in. The collection goes on, and it is well worth a visit.

Southwell

St Andrew's Avalanche Memorial Church, built in 1878, is a memorial to a disaster involving two sailing ships.

The *Avalanche* was on passage to New Zealand with a crew of 34 and 63 passengers. The *Forest* was sailing in ballast to the USA with a crew of 21.

There was a fresh south-westerly gale in the Channel and the seas were rough. Rain and darkness made the visibility bad and there was a collision. The *Avalanche* sank within five minutes and 106 lives were lost – only twelve men from both ships survived.

The bereaved in New Zealand requested that a memorial be erected on Portland as near to the scene of the disaster as was practicable and St Andrew's church is a beautiful memorial to those who perished. At the New Zeland end, in Wanganui, a childrens home for orphans was built to commemorate the disaster and the loss of dear ones. It is interesting to note that parishioners in Southwell still correspond with the governors and wardens of this home, and several New Zealanders have visited Portland and helped financially with church maintenance.

There are beautiful stained glass windows, all dedicated to the deceased, as were all the church fittings. One of the vestry windows incorporates a Maori head, dedicated to the Maori doctor who perished with his son. The bowl-shaped font is also of particular interest, being carved from one large piece of stone. An excellent example of a Portland stonemason's skills.

The original pipe organ was requiring annual maintenance and replacement of parts which proved both costly and unreliable and was therefore replaced by an electric organ in 1975. This revealed a plain glass window previously hidden by the pipes. This window was replaced in 1981. The work was completed in Southwell by a local craftsman. Blue glass divided into seven portions represents the seven seas – vertical strips depicting masts and rigging of sailing ships and 106 clear glass lenses rising up as bubbles – each lens representing a life. This window is known as the centenary window.

During 1984 an amateur diving team stumbled across an unknown wreck in the vicinity of Portland Bill. Items of pottery were recovered and some carried the badge of the Shaw Saville Line. The wreck was definitely identified as that of the *Avalanche*. This pottery is now on display in the church porch. There were also tallow candles, which lit readily and one is lit each year on the anniversary of the disaster.

The diving team became very interested in the church and in 1986 one of the bower anchors from the *Avalanche* was recovered and is now in its permanent resting place in St Andrew's churchyard, together with a plaque detailing the names of the divers who worked on this operation.

Stalbridge

Cadaver tombs are rare. There are said to be only three like the one in Stalbridge parish church in the country. Frederick Treves, in his book *Highways and Byways of Dorset*, first published in 1906, said of it:

'On one altar tomb – so old that all knowledge of its date is lost – is the recumbent figure of a corpse in a shroud. It is a gruesome object, for the body of the unknown is so profoundly emaciated that the ribs appear as entrenchments through the skin. His head reclines on a pillow with roses. What is most noticeable about him is the very determined expression of his mouth, as if on the set lips was the resolve to get no thinner under any possibilities'.

Why was such a tomb erected in this quiet, medieval village which had been probably colonised by the Romans, had a Saxon name and had been mentioned in the Domesday Book but was not remarkable for anything else? It is difficult to say, or to date the tomb with certainty.

Stalbridge's impressive iron town pump stands on The Ring, while the pump house that used to house it stands in Station Road. And, as if that were not confusing enough, The Ring is a triangle. It used to be a bull ring several hundred years ago, so the name stuck. It's a very attractive triangular-shaped piece of grass with high banks to the north and rose beds and a flagpole. At the narrow ends stands the town pump.

Its rather ornate iron work still looks well, though painted green now, and the pump is there for decoration only. Its handle is locked and no water runs there to be drawn up from below.

It had a busy life at the turn of the century though. It was the sole source of water for all the cottages in and around Station Road. The pump house is still in its original place, a most unusual stone building with 'U' shaped scallops between the peaks of the ridge tiles. The high rounded arch above the wooden doors suggests the entrance to a tiny Norman chapel, and the pump house is now a listed building.

Spire Hill used to be called Cooks Lane, with Cooks Farm at the top of it, but after Sir James Thornhill erected his obelisk in 1727 in honour of the accession of King George II, the slope became known as Spire Hill, with Spire Hill Farm to the left of it. Sir James Thornhill had many reasons for gratitude to King George II, his patron, and the Hanoverian Succession generally, for the Hanoverians had given the country stability and prosperity and a climate in which art and architecture could flourish again.

Sir James Thornhill had become famous as the artist chosen to paint the dome of St Paul's, and had been chosen for the work because the Archbishop of his day had insisted on a painter who was first a Protestant and secondly an Englishman. Such was Thornhill's success at this and other commissions that he had been able to buy back the Thornhill estate of his ancestors, sold by a forebear in 1686. The obelisk was blown down in a storm in 1836 but replaced later.

Erecting this obelisk then, clearly visible in the surrounding countryside, must have made plain his Protestant loyalty in a county where some villages, notably Chideock, Lulworth and nearby Marnhull had always been fiercely Catholic.

To the north of St Mary's church lies Stalbridge Park. An ancient grey stone wall ten feet in height encircles the park for a distance of five miles.

The park once contained a beautiful manor house dating from about 1600, which was demolished in 1822. However the old wall and the park gates remained. On either side of the iron gates are two stout ashlar pillars, each surmounted by a lion's head with a fierce expression.

Legend has it that when the nearby church clock strikes midnight, the lions descend to drink at a pool inside the park. On All Hallows Night they are said to rampage through the village of Stalbridge.

Sadly in 1985, two lorries hit the pillars almost causing the lions to topple. In November 1985 the lions were removed by crane, the pillars strengthened and the lions reinstated. Now the church clock no longer strikes and the pool has dried up, but the legend remains.

Stanton St Gabriel

Just over a mile from Chideock and hidden away at the foot of Golden Cap, the highest cliff on the south coast, lies the hamlet once known as Stanton St Gabriel. The area is owned by the National Trust and the old farmhouse and couple of thatched cottages have been beautifully restored for use by summer visitors.

But it is the ruins of the 13th century church which intrigues. Is the story of its beginning fact or fiction?

In the 13th century a ship was battling its way up channel through a dreadful storm. Among those on board was the young wife of the captain.

Fearful that the pounding of the waves and gale force winds would destroy his ship, but more fearful for the safety of his beloved wife, the captain vowed that if she got ashore alive he would build a chapel on that spot in thanksgiving.

As foreseen, the inevitable happened and the ship was lost. Struggling through the waves, the captain was able to get his wife ashore but she died just minutes later.

However she had reached the shore alive so, true to his vow, the captain built St Gabriel's chapel, and its remains are still there for us to see today.

Stock Gaylard

The small church of St Barnabas in the parish of Stock Gaylard is to be found in the grounds of Stock House on the edge of the deer park. In 1884 it was rebuilt from an ivy clad ruin and today is used, occasionally by the villagers of King Stag in north Dorset.

To the south of the nave is the tomb of a Crusader – Sir Ingelramus de Walys, Knight and Lord of the Manor, who went to the Holy Land in the service of King Edward I, and was killed there in 1274. He was rich enough to be able to pay the undertaker in the ancient city of Acre, who specialised in such work, to have his bones sent home in a leather saddle bag. These were found under the hamstone effigy when the church was restored. The recumbent figure of the knight, dating from the late 13th century, lies peacefully, clad in chain mail, his shield slung over his shoulder and his hand resting on the pommel of his sword. His feet are crossed, signifying that he died in the Holy Land, and resting on a lion couchant. His wish that his bones might rest in his beloved homeland, Dorset, has been granted.

To the north of the narrow nave there is another memorial to a more recent crusader. Young Captain Yeatman of the Dorset Yeomanry went to Palestine with Allenby's army in 1918 to liberate the land from the Turks and so, eventually, to open up the way for the formation of the state of Israel. He was shot in the back and killed outside Jerusalem while carrying one of his wounded men to safety. He sleeps in the military cemetery on the hill outside Jerusalem, far from his native land of Dorset, and his kinsmen buried in Stock Gaylard churchyard.

Stourton Caundle

An inscription dated 1977 in St Peter's church tells us that 'In commemoration of the Silver Jubilee of Her Majesty Queen Elizabeth II, the people of Stourton Caundle . . . through happy endeavour and willing subscription, have restored in its original sturdy form the Hour-striking Clock built for the Church by their own Village Blacksmith, John Biddlecombe, 250 years ago . .'

The story began in February 1977, when the newly elected Silver Jubilee Committee decided to look into restoring and bringing back to life the then silent church clock. The clock had not been in operation since 1961, mainly because no-one had taken on the daily task of climbing the tower to wind it!

Despite its long silence, the clock was still in a good condition mechanically. And so began the painstaking task of taking it to bits, restoring and adjusting, and designing new devices to ensure that it ran smoothly and to time.

Electric motors now power the 'going' train for the pendulum and the 'striking' train, so that the clock runs under its own power – and has kept exceptionally good time since Christmas Eve 1977, when it once again came to life.

But the story did not end there, for the clock still needed a clockface. A set of gears and spindles was obtained, made originally for a church in Christchurch, and new brass hands were made in the village. The large hand weighs over five pounds and the small hand over three pounds. They were put in position on 1st July 1978 – the first time the clock had been complete in all its 250 years.

This story of voluntary effort and village endeavour is made more interesting because it was one of Stourton

Caundle's own, the blacksmith John Biddlecombe, who originally made the clock and placed it in the church tower.

The Biddlecombes lived in the village through the 17th and 18th centuries. John, who died in 1741, was probably the first to add the craft of clockmaker to the family trade of blacksmith. It is known that he also made the Purse Caundle church clock, and at least one long-case clock of his make has been found. A hatchment in the church, dedicated to the Biddlecombes, shows the arms and motto of the Worshipful Company of Blacksmiths in London – a sign that this country clockmaker and blacksmith must have been held in high standing by his brother smiths so far away.

Sturminster Marshall

How many readers have whizzed round the roundabout near Sturminster Marshall at the intersection of the A350 with the A31 and wondered why it is known as the Round House Roundabout? Indeed, thousands must pass this way who do not even know its name!

As early as 1766 a turnpike road ran this way from Poole, via Broadstone and Corfe Mullen, and thence on to Blandford. Another turnpike was routed to join it from Hamworthy in 1836, when the junction was known as Bailie Corner. The original Round House was a tollhouse built in 1846 after the upgrading of the old Creepers Lane had formed part of the Piddletown Trust turnpike road.

The first keeper to live in the Round House must have been kept very busy with four roads to watch (towards Wareham/Dorchester, Blandford, Wimborne and Hamworthy), four gates to open and shut and the tolls to collect.

The coming of the railway meant that the tollhouse was redundant within a few years. The last tolls were taken in 1873 and the toll bar removed in 1879.

The Round House then became a private residence and a dame school ('a penny a week, take your own stool')!

An advertisement dated 1902 reads as follows:

'Baillie Old Toll Bar
Mrs Reed
Tea, coffee and refreshments always ready.
A good pull-up for cyclists.'

In the early 1930's it was a cobbler's shop where a George Reeves repaired boots. Mrs Reeves used to make and sell a 'penny monster' of ginger beer.

The Round House was pulled down by 1937 and in 1949 the present roundabout was constructed. Let us hope that the name and this little piece of local history is not quite forgotten, even if there is now no evidence of the site of a building which touched the lives of many local people.

Sugar Hill

On the verge of the road leading from Bere Regis to Wareham at Sugar Hill, is a small white cross; the grass is kept cut and fresh flowers are laid in front of it. Legends abound as to its significance. Is it the grave of a dog unhappily run over? A memorial to a council worker who slipped on the icy road while gritting and died? The unmarked grave of a gipsy child? Or, when the Black Death came into Radipole, did a farmer attempting to get himself and his cattle to safer parts, die of the plague before he could make it!

The truth of the matter is that in 1928 a lorry loaded with tarmac, went out of control struggling up the hill. It collided with a Morris Cowley car driven by a Watford family on holiday. The tail board of the lorry dropped down, tipping hot tarmac over the occupants who had been thrown out of their vehicle. One girl of 14 was so badly burned that she did not survive. Although the record stops here, the council workmen who were involved in the roadworks are said to have erected the cross, and somehow the idea of looking after it has been passed on to the workmen of today.

Swanage

◣ It is recorded in the Domesday Book that Durandus the Carpenter was given the mill at Mowlem for his work at Corfe Castle – Mowlem was one of the manors of Purbeck and could be Swanage, where there is a mill house and mill pond to this day. The mill ceased to function in the middle of the 19th century.

Tithe barn at Swanage, now a museum

Where there is a mill there is a barn to store the corn, and in Swanage on the far side of the church from the mill pond is a fine Purbeck stone barn, built with stone quarried about a mile away. The barn has a stone-tiled roof, graduated in size; the larger tiles just above the walls, known as the verge and jutting out to act as conductors of rain water before the days of gutters.

The barn was built at the end of the 16th century on the site of a much older barn, possibly the same age as the mill. The word tithe denotes that the barn belonged to the church and was where the 'tythe' or tenth of the farmer's produce was taken annually for the upkeep of the church and clergy.

In the walls of the barn are four very narrow tall openings of some three feet in height. These are said to be 'Owl' windows to allow the birds to fly in and hunt the rats which abounded in grain stores.

The tithe barn is now a local museum depicting the history, geology and past trades of Swanage, the stone industry in particular.

Sydling St Nicholas

In the churchyard of this lovely little village, a millstone has been used as a gravestone for a local miller.

The 15th century church of St Nicholas has several unusual and interesting features. The south and west doors are 16th century, and there are still some 18th century box pews. There is an oak chest which is thought to be 13th century. It would have been the parish chest and has three locks – one for each of the churchwardens and one for the vicar. The slot in the top was probably for the receipt of alms or other payments.

The clock, dated 1593, is thought to be the oldest of its kind in England. It has no face but it strikes the hours, using the Sydling bells. The bells are famous for their weight (the tenor weighs over 19 cwts) and for their tone.

There is a chalk stream running through the village and many of its cottages are thatched. High on the downs above the village are the remains of the small rectangular fields cultivated by the Celts long before the Romans came.

Symondsbury

Going westwards out of the parish on the main A35 road, just beyond the old Miles Cross is Angell Knapp. At one time Captain and Mrs Angell lived here in West House.

They bought the house about a month after their marriage, and before Capt Angell returned to sea. When he left she said she would put an oil lamp in the upstairs east window, the light from which could be seen well to the east of Askers Down. In that way he would see a welcoming light when he returned. His ship was lost at sea, no trace of wreckage ever having been found, but for nearly 50 years until her death, the oil lamp was lit and placed in the window.

There is a story too about another local house. A travelling tinker who dealt in scrap metal and old iron did so well he was able to buy a plot of land and have a house built upon it. On adjoining land, the gipsies had parked their caravans for years, but the dealer bought that land also and told the gipsies to leave.

When one gipsy protested, and asked the reason for having to move she was told, 'Because I am going to build a big house here for myself and my descendants.'

The gipsy replied, 'Yes, you will build a fine house here, but your eldest son will never inherit.'

The first house was duly built and insured with several companies, but one weekend – whilst the family were away – a mysterious fire burned it to the ground.

A fine new house was built on the adjoining ground, but up to and including the third generation, the eldest son has never inherited.

Three Legged Cross

➤ The odd name of this village is said to have several origins. One story is that the villagers were having a meeting to decide on a name for their village, when up piped an old lady called Kitty Orman. 'Why not call it Three Cross, zur?', she asked. There are still a few Ormans living in the village today. It is also said that it derived from the meeting of three parishes – Horton, Cranborne and West Parley, which met at a point in Westmoors Road.

Roads have obviously been important to this little settlement. The main road from east to west was the turnpike on which the Duke of Monmouth was taken after he was captured at nearby Horton Heath. This is now a minor road, whilst the road from north to south has become a 'B' road. Gravel excavated from Horton Common and Lower Common was laid to make the early roads. The Travellers Rest public house was always a good resting place for man and beast, the faithful horse being left at the horse trough on the opposite side of the road.

Three Legged Cross was a busy place in years gone by with broom or besom making. With the majority of people having horses and carts, the blacksmith and wheelwright were always in demand. The anvil in the blacksmith's forge still rings out today. Strawberry growing is another occupation which still continues.

Toller Porcorum

➤ Toller Porcorum has had three vicarages. The first and very old vicarage is now the outbuildings of Toller House. The next vicarage was the present Toller House and the third was the recently built St Peter's House.

An old man, a Mr Hansford, now dead for some years, used to tell of by-gone Toller. He said there was an underground passage between the old vicarage buildings and the Old Swan Inn which was immediately across the road. When carts passed between the old vicarage buildings and the inn the iron of the wheels made a hollow sound as they passed over the secret passage.

Recently, when part of the old vicarage buildings was being converted into a cottage, repairs were carried out to the floors. A flight of steps was discovered which went down to a passage, below ground level. This ran in two directions, one towards the Old Swan Inn and the other towards the church. For what purpose was this secret passage built? Most probably for concealing smuggled goods.

For many generations the family of Keech had a tannery in Toller Porcorum. It stood by the little humpty-back bridge over the stream, at the bottom of Toller Lane. Miss Madelane Keech, who died in 1980 aged 88, remembered standing in the lane watching the tannery burn down. There was tallow stored in the roof, and when this caught fire there was no hope of saving the building. She was then 12 years old. Two rooms only of the tannery still survive, incorporated into the present private house. The ground floor room was where the boots were made and gloves were made on the first floor.

The Keeches were an important local family. In the tower of the parish church are four bells. The third has cast into it, 'Mr Richard Keech Churchwarden 1767.'

Before the humpty-back bridge was built there was a ford through the stream. At night, if the stream was in flood, wagoners would call at the tannery and ask to be guided through the stream with a light. In summer, when the woodwork of cartwheels would shrink in the dry heat, carts would be stood in the stream at the ford, to soak and swell the wheels, else their joints came loose.

Trent

➤ Trent is a small village two miles north of the A30, which runs between Yeovil and Sherborne. In the churchyard is a grass-surrounded semi-circular stone inscribed 'Geoffrey Francis Fisher, ninety-ninth Archbishop of Canterbury and Rosamond, his wife'. That the Fishers chose to be buried in this little known village rather than one of the mightiest abbeys of the land is a tribute to the people of Trent, who took them to their hearts when they retired to Trent rectory in 1961. The rectory is surrounded by a stone wall, opposite the church, with a vast cedar and beech tree in the grounds.

Lord Fisher died in Sherborne on Friday 15th September 1972, having been in Trent church, as usual, the previous Sunday, where, as ever, he had a few words with all the parishioners. His funeral was in Trent church on Wednesday 20th September and his memorial service in Westminster Abbey on Tuesday 10th October. The Abbey was packed but a prime place was reserved for the people of Trent, who had set out early to pay their final tribute to their most distinguished incumbent.

An earlier tribute had been made on 5th May 1967 to The Most Reverend Archbishop Lord Fisher of Lambeth and Lady Fisher on the occasion of their Golden Wedding and Lord Fisher's eightieth birthday. The village welcomed them in the village school and the cake was cut. Then the rector presented the village Golden Wedding gift, a teak garden table and four matching chairs inscribed 'Trent – 12.4.67'. The village entertainment was 'An Edwardian Evening'.

Lady Rosamond Fisher was as much admired, loved and respected as the Archbishop, and continued to live in Trent for many years after his death. Her funeral service was also in St Andrew's church.

Geoffrey Francis Fisher, son of a country vicar, was born on 5th May 1887 and educated at Marlborough College. He went on to Oxford where he read Greats, gaining three Firsts in spite of a very active social and sporting life. He returned to Marlborough in 1911 as an assistant master and left at age 27 when he became the headmaster of Repton. He proved a demon for work and yet never seemed fussed. While at Repton he met and married his wife Rosamond and they had six sons.

Priest house dated around 1500 at Trent

From 1932 to 1939 the Reverend Fisher was the Bishop of Chester, where the people of Cheshire soon found that he was not only a fine administrator, but a bishop who was human, who loved the ordinary folk and could talk with kings without losing the common touch. His youngest son was only two years old when he took up this post.

In 1939 he was appointed to the See of London, where he and his wife did sterling work throughout the war-time bombing.

He became Archbishop of Canterbury in 1945, and during his period in office he officiated at Queen Elizabeth II's wedding and coronation.

On his retirement in 1961 he and Lady Fisher moved to Trent where he was the incumbent from 1962 to 1972. There is a permanent display of the Japanese cope and mitre he wore when officiating in the village. On his death these were bequeathed to the Reverend Tim Brook, who has given them to the church.

Trent has had another distinguished resident – in 1651 King Charles II sought refuge in the manor house while fleeing to France after the battle of Worcester. The manor house is on the right of the church, hidden behind a stone wall in spacious grounds, and near to a fine stone-built priest house dated around 1500.

Wakeham (Portland)

Church Ope Cove, Portland, is reached by a short walk off the main road at Wakeham. Passing the small but fascinating thatched museum, the road passes under an arch before descending to a half-circular view point. Wooden seats are provided for those wishing to admire the view rather than take the rather steep path down to the beach.

Overlooking this beautiful spot is the ruined Rufus Castle, which stands on the former site of an edifice called Bow and

Arrow Castle. The latter is believed to have been built during the reign of William II (1087–1100). It was first mentioned when William Malmesbury recorded that Robert, Earl of Gloucester, captured it in 1142 from King Stephen and gave it to the Empress Matilda.

It eventually fell into ruin and during the reign of Henry VI Rufus Castle was built on the site, after Richard, Duke of York, had seized Portland in 1432.

The overhanging parapet at the tops of the walls was used for defence by dropping stones through apertures between the carbels onto troops beneath.

In later years George III handed Rufus Castle over to John Penn (the grandson of William Penn, founder of Pennsylvania) who added an imitation Norman bridge and doorway to the keep. Unfortunately only the pentagonal keep of the castle remains. The walls are seven ft thick and contain circular gun-ports, denoting its importance in the defence of the island.

Below, and to the seaward side of Rufus Castle, a short cliffside path climbs to the church of St Andrew.

Started in the 12th century, the church was built on the site of an earlier Saxon church. Extensions were carried out in the 13th, 14th and 15th centuries, the church reaching its full size by 1475.

For some reason – perhaps its inaccessibility – the church fell into disuse and by 1753 was in ruins. It was finally abandoned in 1756 and part of it was taken to help construct the new church of St George in its stead.

However in 1980–1981 a group working on a Manpower Services Commission scheme restored the remains of this little known church and so helped to preserve some of the history of the Isle of Portland.

Wallisdown

The last inhabitant of the old smuggler's cottage at Wallisdown ended his days in what were then the new almshouses. He was quite a character; children and adults with warts went to him to be cured. He wetted a finger in his mouth, rubbed the warts, mumbled unknown words over them and the spell worked!

Wallisdown has not always been in Dorset. Being on the outskirts of Bournemouth it started off in Hampshire.

The Talbot village school and the church nearby were built by the two Miss Talbots. Their philanthropy did not end there, for there was also a home for the elderly and a boys home, known as Talbot Manor. During the early 1900s the Talbot estate also made scholarship money available to children whose parents wanted them to have more education than they could get at the little village school.

Wallisdown at the turn of the century was a cluster of houses in Park Road (now Alton Road), Priestly Road and Kinson Road. The rest was either heathland or farmland and unmade roads. On the one main road was a well known sight – the Clock House with its large clock in the window, where Mr Hart sat mending clocks and watches. Opposite the Clock House were fields, one of which became the football field and is still the recreation ground of today.

Off Park Road were the lodge gates, the beginning of the private road leading to the home of Lord and Lady Wimborne of Canford. The gates were situated on the 'Drove', as it was known then. It was down this road that they drove cattle bought from Wimborne cattle market to the abattoir at Wallisdown, which is still Hopkins the butcher's. Children were always sent rushing out to make sure the garden gates were shut if the cattle were heard coming.

Wareham

We have become so accustomed to being able to find guide books and county histories covering every conceivable facet of local interest, that it is hard to remember under what difficulties the forerunners of such books were created. Someone, somewhere had to be the first to gather all this information together. One such man, who gave half his life to producing a history of Dorset, is buried in St Mary's church.

John Hutchins was Dorset's first county historian. He was born in 1698 and was a clergyman for some 50 years. He was rector of Holy Trinity, Wareham, until his death in 1773.

He seems to have begun his great work on the prompting of a fellow antiquarian in about 1740. There was an enormous interest in the past amongst many clergymen and gentlemen, and delving into old documents or digging up archaeological remains was a lifelong hobby with many of them. John Hutchins went about his task in a painstaking and surprisingly modern manner. He sent out questionnaires, addressed to the rector or lord of the manor of each village, and asked for help in the great work he was planning.

The amount of work which he brought down upon himself took its toll of his health and strength. Yet despite increasing deafness and, towards the end, partial paralysis, he forged on.

In 1762 a catastrophe nearly ended the work there and then. The Great Fire of Wareham swept through the ancient town on Sunday 25th July 1762. It seems to have started when someone threw hot ashes onto a heap of rubbish and straw. Most of the houses were timber-framed and thatched and the fire spread quickly. Many people lost everything in the four hours it raged. Over 130 houses and buildings were destroyed.

John Hutchins' house was one of those which were burned, and it was only due to the quick action of his wife that his precious papers were saved.

At last, in June 1773, he was ready to write the dedication for his book in preparation to sending it to the printers. Tragically, he died the same month, and was buried at St Mary's. When the book appeared in print the following year, he would have been delighted with the acclaim it received from his peers and the public.

West Bay

➤ Here, where the river Brit runs into the sea, is Bridport's harbour. Despite the difficulties caused by silting up, there has been a port here since the Middle Ages, though the harbour itself was only built in the 1740s.

One family closely connected with the shipbuilding and commercial activities of the harbour were the Goods. William Good was involved in the building of some 16 ships between 1805 and 1814.

Good's Yard's Old Warehouse was built, probably around 1780, to store bales of hemp. It also had a bonded store, with Customs insignia on the door. It is an impressive building with fine vaulted cellars, though it has not been used commercially since the First World War. Outside there still stands an old brick staircase, and the trough where Good's horses used to drink.

Some years ago the sad day came when Reg Good had to bow to modern methods and sell his beautiful shire horses. The teams had been a familiar sight on the beaches, hauling sand and shingle in putts (carts) up the steep ridges. They were followed by mechanical diggers, which scooped out vast loads. However, this was brought to a halt on 30th September 1984, as it was feared removal of shingle at this end of Chesil Beach was causing erosion at the Portland end.

Stone horse trough at West Bay

An entry for 1851 in Hunt and Company's Dorsetshire Directory reads, under Ship Agents, 'Good Daniel, receiver of droits of Admiralty, insurance broker, Custom House, common and general agents, and agent to Lloyd's Bridport Harbour.' The Goods were in fact responsible for establishing the Lloyd's agency here in 1824.

There are some other interesting old houses in West Bay. The Gull's Nest is an attractive house at the end of a narrow passage quaintly known as The Arcade, and is one of the oldest buildings in West Bay. Over the years it has been used as a church, a Sunday school, a meeting hall for the WI, and a post office!

The old Victorian railway station building also still stands – for the moment. The line itself, part of the Bridport Railway Company, was bought by Dorset County Council to build Sea Road, but the station must remind many locals of summer days out at West Bay in their childhood.

West Moors

West Moors can lay claim to its very own martyr. In 1591 William Pike, 'a layman born at Moors in Parley', was executed at Dorchester for his faith, and for denying Elizabeth I's supremacy in the Church.

Pike had apparently been converted to Catholicism by a priest named Pilchard. When he was asked at his execution what had moved him to act as he had done, he was able to reply, with an enviable sense of humour in the circumstances, 'Nought but the smell of a pilchard'! He was hanged, but was taken down before his death for the ritual drawing and quartering. Being a strong man, he continued to resist and finally was effectively crucified on his back by the sheriff's men, who threw him to the ground and pinned him by the hands with their halberds. This terrible story is still remembered in West Moors, and William Pike's ghost is said to walk at a spot in the north of the village.

In the 18th century great improvements took place in the main roads of east Dorset. The Ringwood to Poole and Ringwood to Wimborne roads – which meet at Tricketts Cross – were made across the heath, and the old crossing of the Moors river at Palmer's Ford was abandoned and St Leonard's bridge built farther north. The new turnpike was administered by the Ringwood Trust and the name may still be seen on the roadside milestones.

As well as these turnpikes, which carried the mail coaches and other traffic to and from the larger towns, there were many tracks and footpaths leading from Poole in the west and from Christchurch in the east, over the vast heathland to the north, across Verwood Common to Cranborne, Shaftesbury and Salisbury. These pathways criss-crossed the heath, joining up the farms and villages dotted about this part of Dorset.

The more solitary paths were probably the ones used by the smugglers. In the 18th century smuggling was at its peak and Isaac Gulliver became a wealthy man from 'The Trade'. He owned several houses between Poole and Wimborne and in 1789 acquired Manor Farm in West Moors, which had been built a few years earlier. This was subsequently known as 'Gulliver's Farm' but in the latter half of the 19th century the name was changed to Hatchard's Farm after the man farming it at the time. However, earlier this century it became known, once again, as Gulliver's Farm. Unfortunately, the original farmhouse was burned down in 1935 and only the original barn remains.

Gulliver's oldest daughter married William Fryer, a Wimborne banker. It is possible that some of Gulliver's ill-gotten gains went to support the bank which was finally absorbed by Lloyds. It is also possible that much of the land acquired by the Fryer family in West Moors was the result of inheritance through Gulliver's daughter.

When one thinks of the vast expanse the heathland covered at that time it is not difficult to visualise the smugglers leading their ponies, laden with contraband, along those lonely paths to Salisbury.

West Parley

▬ The ancient church of All Saints is a small picturesque building, consisting of chancel, vestry and north porch. The west end of the nave is surmounted by a wooden bell turret. The churchyard is also attractive and this makes the church very popular for weddings.

The church does not lie from east to west but points to where the sun would rise on All Saints Day before 1752. This was the means of recovering the dedication of the church, which had been lost locally. This was confirmed by later documents. The church stood here in Saxon times and was replaced by the present building in the 12th century – materials being reused from the original building.

The old fashioned pews date from 1841. The square pew is that of the patron and the one next to it is marked 'Choir' and is large enough to accommodate the village musicians who accompanied the singing before organs arrived. Little flap seats may be seen at the ends of some of the pews. These are stools of repentance! Naughty boys were made to sit on these stools if they disturbed the service.

Outside the east wall of the church is a glazed and barred recess with the following inscription –

'Until 1896, when this Chancel was restored, the Urn, said to have held the heart of the Lady of Lydlinch who endowed this Church, lay under the stone on which it now stands.'

144

The Lady of Lydlinch is said to have been the Lady of West Parley Manor, but on her marriage was compelled by her husband to live at Lydlinch. She dearly loved Parley and wished her heart to go there after her death. On her death-bed she made her servants promise to carry out her wish. She is supposed to have endowed the church with her glebe and the tithes of her lands except for part of those from Dudsbury which she reserved for Lydlinch, to which parish they are still paid.

This story is supported by the fact that just outside Lydlinch church is a tomb bearing the inscription 'Here lies the remains of a lady who gave to the rector of this church for ever one portion of the tithes arising out of Dudsbury Farm in West Parley and another out of Knowle Farm in Woodlands'.

Tradition had always stated that the Lady's heart was buried under a flat circular stone five ft two ins outside the old east wall. When the chancel was enlarged the line of the new wall came exactly over the stone. The ground was carefully excavated and three ft from the surface, directly under the middle of the stone, an earthenware urn was revealed. It was a large vessel with traces of greenish glaze. The urn was filled with earth, stony at the top and fine earth below. The 14th century urn is 15 ins tall and 15 ins wide. Eight skulls and many other bones were found buried around the urn.

A sundial with a missing gnomen stands near the entrance gate in the churchyard. This is part of the gallows that stood on Gibbets Firs, East Parley.

On 5th December 1803, William Harbin was buried at Christchurch Priory. He was the owner of a farm on Parley Green and was murdered by his son and son's friend John Guppy. The son was a great disappointment to his father and was to be disinherited. The mother persuaded the son to murder his father before he changed his will. John Guppy, the friend, agreed to help for the princely sum of half-a-crown and at the second attempt successfully killed the father. They were both tried at Winchester and brought back to Gibbets Firs (the place nearest the crime) for execution. The bodies were gibbeted in chains and left to hang for a long time. The mother became insane and spent days and nights scaring away the birds and trying to feed the bodies by throwing potatoes into their mouths.

The owner of the land, disgusted by the sightseers and picknickers, cut down the gibbet and gave part of the post to the rector of West Parley. He set it up where it now stands and placed a sundial on it, which it was said, owing to its dreadful history, never showed the correct time.

Weymouth

➤ Perhaps the strangest scrap of local history is the chilling tale of the ship which put into Melcombe Regis from France in 1348.

Aboard this dark ship was a sailor who carried with him the dreadful infection of the Black Death, which had spread across Europe from central Asia during the previous few years, decimating whole populations in its path. The disease spread quickly in the little port and began its relentless march through England. Once it had entered the rat population, nowhere was safe. Bubonic plague, with its grotesque black swellings, killed within three to five days; even quicker was pneumonic plague, which attacked the lungs and killed in two days. By late 1348 the plague had reached London, and 1349 can with justice be called England's 'Plague Year'. Whole villages disappeared and the land was left untilled. No-one can say for certain how many people died, but estimates vary between a third and a half of the entire population. It was indeed a Ship of Death which put into little Melcombe Regis.

Amongst the treasures of St Mary's, the parish church in

St Mary's Street, is a painting of the Last Supper. The artist was Sir James Thornhill, who was born in Melcombe Regis in 1675. His portrait hangs in the nearby Guildhall, as does that of his contemporary, Sir Christopher Wren.

Thornhill became a prominent artist of the early 18th century, and his commissions included work for Queen Anne at Hampton Court and Windsor, and for the great houses of Chatsworth and Blenheim. He also painted portraits, including one of the notorious rogue, Jack Sheppard, who was hanged at Tyburn in 1724. Perhaps his greatest work, though, was on the dome of St Paul's Cathedral.

One of Thornhill's pupils was William Hogarth, destined to be a great painter and engraver in his own right. Unfortunately Sir James' early patronage was ill rewarded when in 1729 Hogarth eloped with, and married, his daughter.

Thornhill had been knighted by George I in 1720. However he did not forget his home town, and became MP for Melcombe Regis in 1722. He died in 1734.

It was later in the century that Weymouth, as opposed to the original port of Melcombe Regis, attained its present day royal atmosphere. George III liked the little resort so much when he visited it in 1789 that he and his family stayed ten weeks. They returned regularly for several years in succession. The marks of that royal favour are everywhere in Weymouth today, from the white horse cut into the downs behind the town, complete with George III in a cocked hat, to the proud statue at the junction of the town's main streets.

Royal patronage had an odd side effect on the town. It might be thought that the presence of the King – who was after all the head of the British Government – would put a damper on illegal activities, especially smuggling. Far from it. The King's visits seem instead to have had the reverse effect. Smuggling in Weymouth took on an unusually seasonal cycle, at its height when the King was 'in residence'.

The reason of course is that it was not just the King and his family who came to stay. With them came the court officials, the servants, the courtiers and the hangers-on, not to mention the sight-seers who came to catch a glimpse of the Royal Family. The town's population grew by thousands almost overnight. And who was better placed to satisfy the demand for extra tea, tobacco, brandy and wine – as well as the luxuries such as playing cards, silks and coffee – than the smugglers? Few questions were asked when it was a case of satisfying the needs of the town's most illustrious visitor.

So there is in Weymouth not only evidence of its royal past, but also of its lawless past. There are still some of the old smuggling inns, such as the Black Dog, where a Revenue Officer was killed while trying to arrest a smuggler. King George was undoubtedly aware of what went on in the harbour and on nearby beaches, but turned a benignly blind eye. It would be interesting to know the feelings of his Revenue men, who so often put their lives in danger to uphold the King's law against smuggling!

Wimborne Minster

➤ This lovely little town possesses many treasures. A nunnery was founded here in the 8th century, which began the long association with the church. Nothing now remains of the later ecclesiastical buildings except the church, which was restored twice in the 19th century.

Do take the time to explore the Minster. One of its treasures is a little out of the way.

To reach the Chained Library in Wimborne Minster, a narrow winding staircase leads to the Muniment Room where the contents are housed. The library was founded in 1686 for the free use of the citizens of Wimborne and most of the books are chained to the walls, but some of the more notable ones are kept under glass in the centre of the room.

There is a Breeches Bible of 1595 and Raleigh's *History of the World*, written in 1618. A hole was burned through some hundred pages, but all have been carefully repaired. A Matthew Prior is reputed to have been the culprit through falling asleep while reading by the light of a candle, which toppled over.

There are some medieval documents with seals, and 14th century manuscripts on vellum. Also on display are churchwardens' accounts from 1403 to 1474, and a collection of church music – copies of which are in the British Museum. Although exposed to sunlight and storage in damp conditions, the ink on the churchwardens' accounts has lasted throughout the centuries.

There is included in the exhibition an alms box for silver coins, as copper ones were too coarse to go through the narrow aperture, a case of coins, fragments of pottery and a pewter vessel for holding anointing oil.

Winterborne Stickland

➤ The village of Winterborne Stickland lies in a valley in the north Dorset downland. This is an ancient landscape and has long been settled. On the downs at Wimborne Houghton are the remains of two Romano–British settlements and in Turnworth, to the north of Winterborne Stickland, there is a well preserved prehistoric and Roman settlement.

Winterborne Houghton is the source of the stream that flows down through Stickland during the winter months, once the longest millrace in the county. Now there is a waterfall where the waterwheel once turned.

The villages are expanding rapidly but they still retain a core of attractive thatched cottages grouped around their flint churches. The land is mainly put to dairy and sheep farming, although parts of the downland have been planted with trees. These woods create a more sheltered environment in contrast to the windswept downs.

The peace of these woods must often have been shattered during the Second World War. In late 1940, the country was hourly expecting an invasion as Hitler massed his troops on the other side of the Channel. By then, the defence of the land was in the hands of the Royal Air Force. Dorset had several fighter stations covering the county. It was from one such station at Warmwell that a Spitfire took off on 29th November 1940.

When it reached the north Dorset downs it was flying very low. It finally flew into Durweston Forest on the outskirts of Winterborne Stickland, crashing into the trees and killing the young pilot. John Frederick Woodward Allen, from 152 Fighter Squadron, was just 19 when he died.

A memorial tablet was placed on a tree at the site of the crash and, on 10th February 1959, another tablet was attached to the same tree in memory of Pilot Officer Allen's father. He too had been a member of the RAF, and his ashes were scattered where his son's aircraft had come down.

A small area was cleared and planted as a memorial. The Allen family gave spring bulbs. Captain Portman gave flowering shrubs and trees and a delightful garden was created 'In grateful and respectful memory of Pilot Officer John Frederick Woodward Allen'.

Many years later it was realised that the 'memorial' tree had died and that the deer of the forest were using it as a rubbing post. The tablets were in danger of being lost. At a ceremony on 9th April 1978, the RAF Association of Blandford replaced the dead tree with a plinth of polished granite, to which the refurbished tablets were fixed.

Those who walk in the forest will find in the depths of Field Grove this peaceful garden, a hidden memorial to a father and his son, who died defending his country.

Part of the Nine Stones ring at Winterbourne Abbas

Winterbourne Abbas

➤ Along the road from Bridport to Dorchester, just as you reach the village of Winterbourne Abbas, can be found the Nine Stones.

This circle of nine standing stones is of ancient origin and may have been connected with some form of worship. There are seven small stones and two larger ones, within a diameter of about 25 ft. This area has an enormous number of burial mounds and round barrows. Pevsner records a long barrow, 44 round barrows at Poor Lot some two miles away, and another 41 barrows in the parish as a whole.

Local people imbue the stones with strange powers. Twice in the 1980s they are said to have caused vehicles passing by to have suddenly become immobile, all the electrics in the cars suddenly cutting out.

On both occasions the young men concerned became alarmed because it is an unlit stretch of road and there was some danger of other vehicles crashing into them while they were stationary. After frantically searching under the bonnet for some cause for the breakdown, the engines just as suddenly came to life again.

Apparently these or similar occurrences happen about every ten to 20 years. Local people believe the stones are responsible. Is it magic or magnetic?

Woodlands

➤ Just off the road from Cranborne to Wimborne, approaching a village called Woodlands, stands an enormous oak tree of great age. Thought to be more than 400 years old, parts of the trunk are hollow, but huge branches are very much alive and flourishing.

There is a small brass plaque by the tree, polished every day by the lady who lives in the cottage opposite. This states that in 1551, Edward VI sat beneath this tree and touched for the King's Evil. Such events are rare, and certainly seldom recorded.

The young King Edward VI, son of Henry VIII, was visiting Poole, when plague broke out. He was removed to a safer place, Wilton House, home of William Herbert, Earl of Pembroke. As was customary, a hunt was arranged for his entertainment in Cranborne Chase, but somehow or other he became separated from the main party and stopped to rest under an oak tree.

As soon as the local inhabitants heard that the King was there they thronged about him, to be touched for disease and therefore cured. Where this idea came from is not known or understood, but people certainly believed it. The disease known as King's Evil is now thought to be scrofula, some form of tuberculosis of the skin. What would have happened to the young King had he not been found by his host, gives considerable alarm, but he was found and joined by the main party.

The great oak tree, since that time, has been called Remedy Oak.

Wyke Regis

The church of All Saints in this old fishing village was once the mother church of Weymouth. The village's royal connection goes all the way back to AD 988, when Ethelred II granted the village of 'Wyck' to one of his ministers.

Built of Portland stone, the church was dedicated in 1455. It is an impressive building and helps to retain the identity of Wyke Regis now that Weymouth has crept out to meet it. It has, of course, intimate associations with the sea and seafaring folk.

Mackerel fishing was a local industry for centuries. After hours or sometimes days of waiting, a message might come that the shoals were in sight. A general rush to the beach would follow, boats were speedily launched and great hauls were often brought in. When the boats put out from Wyke Regis, the old women used to assemble at 'Passage', to meet them on their return and to pack all the fish into hampers.

But those who lived by the sea were all too aware of its dangers. A memorial stone stands against the church wall, recording that in 1815 the East Indiaman *Alexander* was wrecked in the bay. One hundred and forty crew and passengers (some women and children) were buried here, and this was by no means the only such mass burial. There is also a memorial to a smuggler, 'William Lewis, killed by a gunshot wound' on 21st April 1822. In 1824 the rector of Wyke Regis watched as a tidal wave hit Chesil Beach, sweeping away 80 houses and destroying the villages of Fleet and Chesil. Twenty six people died that day.

The church bells were in a sad state of repair until the villagers banded together in 1988 to celebrate their millenium, and donated the proceeds of a week of festivities to the Bells Restoration Fund. In 1791 the bells had been rung for a visit by George III, and the thirsty bellringers were rewarded with five shillings beer money. Now the bells can ring again as sweetly as before. The tenor bell weighs three quarters of a ton and bears the inscription:

'Lord may this bell forever be
A tuneful voice o'er land and sea,
To call they people unto thee'

Before leaving the church, spare a thought for the harassed parish clerk who many years ago gave out this notice— 'I be desired to gie notice there 'ull be no Sunday here next Sunday 'cos Parson be goin' to preach at Broadmayne, and I be further desired to gie notice there 'ull be a meeting at the Fisherman's Arms to determine what colour the church shall be whitewashed.'

Yetminster

Like any other church clock, the clock of St Andrew's chimes the hours across the village, but unlike most it has no face. It is said that this is because the parishioners could not agree on which side of the tower to place it.

It was made by Thomas Bartholomew of Sherborne in 1682. The church books record much expenditure on cleaning, oiling and repairing. For instance –

| 1746 | 2 new ropes for the clock | | 7s. | 0d. |
| | Thos Maidment for looking after the clock | £1 | 0s. | 0d. |

154

1751	Ralph Cloud for doing the clock and chimes	£2	7s.	0d.
	He required a pint of Sweet Oyl		1s.	6d.
	(Ralph Cloud came from a Beaminster family of clock-makers)			

In Jubilee year, 1897, the clock was overhauled and a carillon mechanism was added, a gift from the wealthy and generous Mr Arthur Scott Williams of Hill House. Strings from the clock were made to operate hammers which tap the bells at three, six, nine and twelve o'clock, playing *God save the Queen* (on only five bells and sadly out of tune). It was first heard on Queen Victoria's Diamond Jubilee Day at three o'clock, when Mr Williams himself started the mechanism and 'amid the breathless silence of the large congregation' the national anthem rang out. Almost without interruption it has done so every three hours since that day, reminding the village still of Queen Victoria's Jubilee.

But from March to October 1986, the clock was silent. After 300 years of daily winding, when the last sexton, Mr Jim Ellis, became too old to climb the steep turret stairs every day, the PCC decided to launch an appeal for automatic winding to be installed. The work was enthusiastically carried out by Mr Wardle of Wylye and, after a few teething troubles, has been entirely successful. Yetminster again has its faceless, patriotic chiming clock. Visitors are astonished and sometimes wonder whether they should stand to attention, but the inhabitants of Yetminster like the unusual manner in which they are reminded of the passage of time.

On the south wall of the church is a splendid brass monument to Sir John Horsey of Clifton Maybank and his wife Elizabeth. Sir John died in 1531, but the date of Elizabeth's death is left blank (Thomas Hardy wrote a long story-poem about her).

We know that Sir John had a hand in the rebuilding of the

nave at the end of the 15th century, and he bequeathed 40 shillings a year for the upkeep of the church in return for prayers for his soul. But soon came the Reformation and willingly or unwillingly the Church had to submit to dictation from the Crown. It is ironical that Sir John Horsey's grandson (another John) was one of Edward VI's commissioners who visited Yetminster church in 1555 to make sure that the churchwardens had obediently obliterated all signs of popery.

Nevertheless, we can still see on the Horsey brass the words 'Lady helpe' and 'Jesu mercy', which would have been offensive to Puritans, who disapproved of prayers for the dead. The brass thankfully escaped the saint-bashers. It was restored and placed on the wall in 1890 by Major Ralph Edward Horsey.

Upbury Farm is the oldest house in the neighbourhood, a rare example of a well-preserved 15th century open hall house. It is obviously a house built for somebody important and well-to-do. It must have been the manor house of Yetminster Upbury (one of four manors into which Yetminster was divided in 1091).

The most remarkable tenant farmer was Benjamin Jesty (1737–1816), known to be among the first to practise vaccination (from Latin vacca – a cow). It had long been observed by country people that dairymaids, having caught the mild cowpox from sick cows, were immune from smallpox, and some experiments on people had been made. In 1774 smallpox broke out in Yetminster. Jesty's two dairymaids nursed their sick relatives without falling ill. He decided to immunize his wife and two small sons by scratching their arms with lymph taken from the udder of a sick cow with a stocking needle. His wife was alarmingly ill but recovered and all three were later proved immune from smallpox. In spite of much public derision he continued to vaccinate. The family moved to Worth Matravers in 1796.

In that same year Dr Edward Jenner, after years of

research, made his first vaccination and was publicly honoured as the first vaccinator. Benjamin Jesty's courageous experiment, predating Jenner's by 22 years, was only brought to public notice because he met Dr Bell of Swanage, a vaccination enthusiast, who wrote to the Vaccine Pock Institute in London. The result in 1805 was an invitation to Benjamin Jesty to visit London, all expenses paid. With some reluctance he agreed to go, was received with honour and had his portrait painted.

Dr Jenner is usually credited with having discovered vaccination. Neither he nor Jesty discovered or understood it. They both followed a tradition common in cattle-breeding parts of the country and experiments that country people had made. Jesty was a farmer while Jenner was a scientist capable of rational experiments and published his results.

Index

The Dorset Federation of Women's Institutes is composed of 184 Institutes throughout the County, varying in size, some rural, some urban. Meetings take place once a month and can be held in the morning, afternoon or evening. There are also 15 W.I. Markets which are open once a week. Should you need more information, the staff at County Office, Princes Street, Dorchester, telephone 0305-266366 will be very willing to help.